AN
EXCELLENT
LIFE

How True and Lasting
Success is Achieved

DARRELL THOMAS

Performance Publishing Group
McKinney, TX

ISBN: 978-1-956914-47-4

DEDICATION

This book is dedicated to my
wonderful wife, Ingrid.

———⁓⊙⦿⊙⦿⊙⦿⊙⊙⁓———

I want to thank the following people
who contributed to this book.

Ingrid Thomas, Brandi Julian, Helena Groves,
Leon Levine, Robbi Fischer, Janet Fischer.
Jonathan Scott, Jim Howard, Chris Howard,
Courtney Donaldson, Michelle Prince, the rest of the
Performance Publishing Team, Howard Partridge,
Tom Ziglar, Laurie Magers, Scott Zack,
Santiago Arango, and Bruce "BRB" Barbour.

I thank & appreciate you all.

Darrell can be reached at
darrell@anexcellentlife.info

CONTENTS

FOREWORD

**"Success is the maximum utilization
of the abilities God gave you."**

As a little boy I remember asking Dad, "If someone lives out what the Bible teaches like in the 10 Commandments, will they be successful in life even if they don't believe in God?" Dad said, "Of course they will, but I can only wonder how much more successful they would have been if they had believed at all."

No matter where you are on your journey, I believe An Excellent Life will help you. You are about to experience 22 succinct and powerful chapters that will each move you one step closer to a more balanced and successful life. The advice is life-changing, but even more important is the thinking behind the advice. This makes the book easy to digest and implement, no matter your background and experience.

What does success mean to you? Do you believe success happens by chance, or by choice? Is success measured by words or actins? If the most important person in your life came to you and asked, "How do I become successful and leave a legacy that ripples throughout eternity?", would you tell them to do what you say, or what you did?

An Excellent life is about living and doing. I have known Darrell for many years and I can tell you he leads by example and through his service to others. Dig into this book and get ready to take your life to the next level.

Tom Ziglar, CEO of Zig Ziglar Corporation

INTRODUCTION

WHAT would you consider to be an excellent life? What would that look like? Does the question make you think of anyone specific? Maybe it makes you think of a business or political leader who possesses power, charisma, and influence. Maybe it makes you consider the life of a famous athlete or celebrity who has millions of fans and an endless fortune. When you think of your own life, do you think an excellent life is about being happy and content, or is it about having a highly successful career with material possessions and the respect and admiration of others?

Past generations understood that a successful and excellent life was simply not possible without developing and living out certain positive virtues. Honesty, integrity, and positive character were not only commonplace but expected. In today's society, this has sadly been replaced by the view that we should somehow be able to choose our own version of morality.

Truth, once considered absolute, is now up for interpretation, and what is considered to be right or wrong produces intense debate. As a result, anyone with well-defined values is often dismissed as being intolerant and non-inclusive. Over time, we have radically altered our view of what is considered to be acceptable behavior. We have, in fact, turned into a society that finds it difficult to judge anyone for anything, no matter how wrong we may know it to be.

This has caused a vast division in our society which is being played out in our everyday lives and at the highest levels of business, government, and religion. As a result, America, and indeed the world find themselves at a tipping point.

It is my hope the pages to come will inspire us to take a deep and intimate look at ourselves and how our lives and the world around us can be radically improved by focusing on positive virtues, such as truth, honor, courage, integrity, self-discipline, and building positive moral character. *An Excellent Life* encourages us to rethink what we believe we know about who we are, how true and lasting success is achieved, and what is truly most important in all of our lives.

As you continue to read, it will become obvious that I am a person of faith, but understand that I will not be bombarding you with "religion" in this book. In fact, when I first sat down to write, it was my specific intention to avoid making this about my faith, but I soon realized this would be impossible. I say it would be impossible because everything I do with my life and every decision that I make is filtered and directed by my belief in God and the knowledge that He loves each of us and has a plan for our lives.

There is simply no other way for me to tell this story because the very foundation of everything I have learned and know about how to live a successful and excellent life is a direct result of the relationship I have with God and faithfully implementing the lessons He teaches.

As the pages unfold, you will see how a few fundamental principles and lessons are essential to achieving and living an excellent life. Some may skim over or completely overlook these lessons, perhaps because they seem so simple that we think we already know them… but do we really? They are very much "common sense" lessons, and yet, when focused upon, studied, dissected, fully understood, and put into practice, we will discover they are very powerful, transformational, and absolutely life-changing.

You see, even if you aren't a Christian believer, you still have to live your life with certain values and virtues, or it will be very difficult—if not impossible—to live an excellent life. I mean, you have to believe in working hard, or you will never achieve your goals. You have to believe in treating other people fairly and honestly, or any success you achieve will be short-lived. You have to believe in telling the truth and treating others with respect, or you won't win. You have to live a life of integrity and continually build your character, or it will be difficult to achieve any real or lasting success.

So, what exactly is success? Since success may be defined in many different ways, let's look at this right up front. To most people, success is exclusively about the attainment and accumulation of money, honors, or high position. I have asked literally hundreds of people what their definition of success is, and quite frankly, most have no idea how to define it, but it usually has something to do with being "rich" and or "famous."

In its most basic form, success is simply the realization of a predetermined goal, but there is obviously much more to it than that. It is not difficult to understand that someone can be *financially successful* and actually live a very *miserable* life. Thus, I believe that true success is about living a *balanced* life. It is about loving, honoring, and serving God, having a close and loving family, having quality relationships with friends and neighbors, as well as achieving lasting, sustainable prosperity in a way that meets all of our *needs*, not necessarily our *greed's*. The mystery seems to be in how we accomplish this.

To me, one of the greatest tragedies in life is that it takes us so long to learn life's lessons, that is if we ever learn them at all. I am writing this as a father who, like all of you who have children, wants nothing but the best for them. We want our children to grow up happy, financially free, and feeling completely fulfilled. No one wants their children to face hardships, trials, and struggles to learn the same hard lessons of life the way we did. We want them to be confident in who they are so they can successfully navigate the evolving landscape of life and achieve any goals and dreams they may hold in their hearts.

Sounds simple, right? Well, it is simple, but it is far from easy. The real question is *why isn't it that easy?* If I, as a father, have learned what it takes to navigate life's challenges, then why can't I simply share what I have learned with my children in a way they can understand and learn for themselves? The answer is as obvious as it is regrettable. It is because every single one of us is infected from conception with an unavoidable plague known as *free will.*

You can tell a child, "Don't run with the scissors, don't eat the soap, don't poop in the bathtub, don't, don't, don't..." and do they do these things anyway? Of course, they do. The sad fact is that kids who run with the scissors often turn into teenagers who experiment with sex, alcohol, and drugs and consequently turn into adults who end up in bad relationships and continually struggle with life. Then they wonder why life is so hard, ultimately, in many cases, living lives of quiet desperation or worse.

In addition, today we find ourselves with infinitely more distractions and ways to divide our attention than any preceding generation, and it seems that around every corner, we are introduced to a new set of challenges to understand, navigate, and solve.

These include technology-induced distractions, such as cell phones, the internet, texting, social media, email, and who knows what is next. Through our devices, we are continually updated on the latest news from every corner of the world. We find ourselves continually adapting to an endless wave of information, new technology, and innovation.

For example, the amount of information we possess as a society throughout history would typically double about every one hundred years. After World War II, it began to double every twenty-five years. At its current rate, the amount of information we possess is doubling every thirteen months. Researchers now tell us that because of the volume of information available to us via the internet, as well as its ease of access, information will soon be doubling at a staggering rate of every twelve hours. And it is all coming at us from the palms of our hands.

While in many ways these advancements have made life easier, better, more convenient, and more productive, we also find that our thoughts, and thus our focus is incrementally scattered and systematically divided. This is because all of this incoming information has nearly unlimited access to our attention and minds, and, therefore, our lives. The danger is that we gradually lose sight of, or never fully develop, the most basic fundamentals of life that actually do lead to happiness, meaningful relationships, contentment, financial independence, and a successful, excellent life.

Have you ever wondered why some people are so incredibly successful? Why is it that some people are truly happy and financially free while others struggle and eek by in life, living out lives of quiet desperation? What makes truly successful people so different? What are the common denominators they share? Have you ever wondered why some seemingly successful people ultimately sabotage their lives, often in very tragic ways? It is actually all very predictable.

This book is about building character, gaining self-awareness, improving self-confidence, and restoring hope and wisdom. It is about eliminating fear, anxiety, worry, pride, jealousy, and envy. It is also about redemption, forgiveness, love, and grace. I share with you my own experiences and observations and blend them with the wisdom of the Bible and the teachings of Albert Einstein, Earl Nightingale, Dr. Martin Luther King, Jr., John Maxwell, Zig Ziglar, Jim Rohn, C.S. Lewis, and many others.

When I say I will use my experiences, I mean the journey I took as a thirty-five-year-old man, having just moved to Charlotte, North Carolina, with no place to live, not a friend or family member within 250 miles, and only $35 to my name. It is about how, by taking one tiny incremental step at a time, I was able to transform my life from being stressed out, miserable, and broke to experiencing joyful, sustainable, and predictable success.

Today, I am a successful debt-free business owner, entrepreneur, and author. I have a truly beautiful and godly wife, two wonderful daughters, and an amazing granddaughter. I am literally living the life of my dreams, and it is one hundred percent because I have implemented the principles detailed in this book.

This is a no-frills, plain-spoken, common sense, no holds barred, from the gut, "check-up from the neck up" that, if you follow, will help you learn what is holding you back and keeping you from achieving the goals you have established for your life.

The information contained in this book is the key that helped me unlock and cast aside the chains that had shackled my life for so many years and led me step-by-step to successful achievement.

The purpose of this book is to help you, as an intelligent person who has already experienced some of, or maybe even a lot of life's hardships, to better navigate the seemingly endless hurdles of life, and to set you firmly on the path leading to long-term success, happiness, and, ultimately, an excellent life.

I want you to know that what you are about to read is written from the heart. The implementation of the information you are about to discover changed my life and will achieve the same results for you, if you will follow its direction. It is my sincere hope and prayer that we can take this journey together, arm in arm and page by page.

Chapter 1
The "Dash"

I WILL always remember the day my grandfather died. It was the summer I was ten. My brother, sister, and I had been water skiing with our father at Lake Lanier, just north of Atlanta. We had finished skiing and were headed back home when a Georgia state trooper pulled my father over. My dad got out of his green Chevy C10 pick-up and approached the trooper. They spoke for a minute or so, and my dad returned to the truck. I could tell by how quiet my dad was that something was wrong, but without comment, we continued toward home. Shortly after we arrived, our parents told us about our grandfather's death.

My grandfather was a product of World War I, World War II, and the Great Depression. He had six sons, including my father, and was married to my grandmother for fifty-six years. He earned his living as a carpenter and farmer and raised his family in a very modest home just outside of Atlanta. He never attended college and was not a financially wealthy man, although, at his funeral, I would come to realize just how truly rich he actually was.

> *Better is a poor man who walks in his integrity*
> *than a rich man who is crooked in his ways.*
> *—Proverbs 28:6*

As a ten-year-old boy, I hadn't attended many funerals. I recall walking into the funeral home with my parents and my brother and sister in tow. We were early for the service, and yet, it was quite crowded. I was astonished by the number of flowers; they were everywhere. I began to count the wreaths and arrangements, but there were just too many. The flowers were neatly layered, one atop another, so it was hard to tell where one arrangement ended and the next began.

As I walked around the funeral home, it seemed as if the entire town was there. I overheard a funeral home employee say he had never seen so many people at a service before. People I had never met were telling stories about my grandfather. I heard comments about how kind he was, what a great friend he was, how he had been such a strong member of the church and local community. There were tears in the eyes of some and belly laughs from others. Hearing the countless stories about the life of my grandfather, I walked away from this experience knowing in my heart that living a life of honesty, integrity, and character was infinitely more important than having money.

After the funeral, life returned to normal, the summer ended, and fall began. At some point, my parents took us back to the gravesite. As my parents made their way to my grandfather's grave, I wandered around looking at all the tombstones. As I looked at one and then the next, I noticed how each tombstone was different. Some had crosses, some were tall, some were short, and others looked like giant monuments. I read the different names, dates, and inscriptions on the tombstones. Some were recent while others were quite old. I tried to find something all of the tombstones shared in common, but there was nothing. After a while, I found my parents standing before my grandfather's grave. As I remembered why we were there, my mood changed, and then I noticed my grandfather's tombstone. It was polished granite with a freshly carved inscription. I finally realized what all the tombstones had in common. It was the *dash*. To this day, I cannot recall a single word on my grandfather's tombstone; I just remember focusing on that tiny little dash.

As Linda Ellis so eloquently points out in her poem, "The Dash" is the small line between a person's date of birth and their date of death. The dash is the most overlooked part of a tombstone, and yet is by far the most important. How can a little dash on a person's tombstone be so important? It is important because it represents the entire *life* of the deceased. Every single event, every birthday, every relationship, every challenge or setback, every success, and indeed every single day of a person's life is summed up on their tombstone by that simple little dash. The question is not *if* we will have a dash; the question is what our dash will represent. This brings up life's most important question: What will *you* do with *your* dash?

The Big Idea

- Having money does not equal "success."
- Live with integrity.
- What will *your* dash represent?

Chapter 2
What Will You Do with Your Dash?

"The world as we have created it is a process of our thinking.
It cannot be changed without changing our thinking."
–Albert Einstein

THE title of this book is *An Excellent Life*. When you think about the word *excellent*, do you feel this word applies to you and the way you have lived your life so far?

The purpose here isn't to beat you up or to, in some way, point out or magnify any shortcomings you may have, and we are not in any way talking about perfection. The best we can ever expect to achieve as human beings is to do our absolute most with the talents, abilities, and gifts we have been given. The vast majority of us conduct our lives with good intentions, and we truly want to be and do our very best.

We all come into this world naked, crying, and confused, and while the naked and crying part might improve, we tend to continue being confused because, let's face it, life can be *very* confusing, and it can be difficult at times to know which road to follow. It seems we all instinctively know the difference between right and wrong, but as life progresses, the lines between right and wrong often become a bit fuzzy. Why is that? The fact is that our culture is structured in this way. We can talk with our parents or go to church and get one message and then we read a book, go to a movie, or talk with a friend and get a completely different, even competing, message.

Psychologists tell us that our behavior tends to be learned through *modeling*—or observing others. Meaning that through observation, we learn to imitate the actions and behaviors of those around us. We pick up how we speak, our manners, our use of language, and the way we act and interact with others in general, both positive and negative, through observing the actions and behavior of others. Others include parents, teachers, siblings, friends, and even people from television, movies, and games. Every aspect of our behavior, and thus our character, is influenced and formed in this way.

Most people will say there are a few very basic and generic things they want out of life. We all want to be happy, healthy, and prosperous. We want a life of peace and security. We want to have good friends and a loving family. We want to have hope for the future, and we all want to be loved and treated with respect. These are all very basic things, and yet, I believe that nearly everyone would agree that someone who had all of these things in life could be said to have had "an excellent life." Sadly, however, most people do not have all of these things in their lives, or at least not to the degree or extent they would like... but why not?

When asked about what they want out of life, most people can list a few things, but they usually need a little prompting to produce a complete list, and this exposes the problem. The vast majority of people don't really know what they want out of life, and if they do know, they seldom have an actual concrete plan to achieve it. In most cases, it breaks down kind of like this: a surprisingly small percentage of people really do know what they want out of life, and they are diligent and focused on achieving those things. They tend to be people who have learned from others the importance of setting goals and having a plan in place to accomplish them. They are usually people who have had mentors in their lives and have actually seen, through the lives of others, the value of knowing *what* they want and, more importantly, knowing *why* they want it. It is this small percentage of people who are fully and diligently focused on the most important areas of their lives, and they have a specific and detailed plan to accomplish their goals.

Of the remaining vast majority, some know what they want, but they have no definite plan to achieve it. Still others within this majority don't really know what they want at all. They just know they want things to be *different* or *better*, and so their plan is to *hope* or *wish* for things to improve, which is, in effect, the same as having no plan at all.

The hard fact is that most people spend more time planning their wedding than they do planning their marriage and more time planning a vacation than they do planning their *lives*. We kind of "wing it" instead of actually drafting a plan. Without even giving it any real thought, we, by default allow others to do our thinking and choosing for us instead of taking control of our lives and knowing for ourselves *what* we want and *why* we want it.

It is vital to understand that the person who truly lives an excellent life is the one who courageously, intentionally, and *deliberately* chooses for themselves the life they want to lead, and they do this based on their own deeply held personal beliefs and values. They do not look to others to know *what* they believe. They form their *own* opinions based on their *own* beliefs, values, and political and biblical worldviews.

Never allow yourself to fall into the trap of believing that politicians, the news media, or the so-called "intellectual elite" know better how to plan and carry out your life than you do. Never assume that just because someone has an MBA or PhD after their name or a microphone or television camera in front of them that somehow this person is more intelligent or more informed than you, thus believing their opinions to be somehow more enlightened, more correct, or more valuable. We need to have a deep, fundamental understanding of our *own* core beliefs and know beyond any doubt exactly where these beliefs come from and precisely *why* we have them.

Let me ask you a question. Do you want to have an excellent life? Do you really? Do you want to know *how* to have an excellent life? Well, ironically, it is much *simpler* than you may think and even more *difficult* than you could ever possibly imagine.

So, what is this elusive secret? Well, get ready to write this one down or grab the highlighter...

The secret to living an excellent life is to live with *intention*.

Know that an excellent life can only be achieved by intentionally and deliberately choosing the kind of life you want to live and knowing without question *why* you want it.

What could possibly be simpler? Once this is done, you form a detailed plan to accomplish what you desire and then you go out and do it, *intentionally!*

Understand that being excellent at anything in life is never achieved without *intention*, and excellence in any form doesn't just happen. Excellence is never a random event. Excellence can only be achieved by diligent and disciplined effort and is pre-meditated, pre-planned, and achieved on purpose.

Here is what I mean. If you get a college degree, it is because you *intended* to get a college degree. You don't get a college degree without a plan and without following through on that plan. If you save money, it is because you *intended* to save money. If you earned a promotion at work, it is because you had a plan, worked hard, disciplined yourself, and set about achieving it because that is what you *intended*. If you build your character, it is because you understand the benefit of building, expanding, and developing the qualities that make you a better person, and you make it a priority to work on yourself *intentionally*. If you want a happy and fulfilling family life, this doesn't just happen by chance or in some random way; you have to work toward that, specifically and *intentionally*. If you want to be in great physical shape, you do so *intentionally* and deliberately through continuous and sustained effort. Anything you want in life that you deem positive and productive can only be accomplished by *intentionally* and *deliberately* seeking it out and working hard to achieve it. As soon as we say, "Oh well... it will work out somehow," the random nature of life wins out, we don't meet our goals, we don't achieve our dreams, and unfortunately, this is what the overwhelming majority of us actually do.

When I say, "It is simpler than you may think," I mean all you have to do is decide *what* you want, know *why* you want it, form a plan, and go do it. When I say, "It will be more difficult than you could ever possibly imagine," this is because it will mean changing the way you *think* and thus, changing your *habits*, and changing your habits will take dedicated day-by-day, long-term effort and *intentional* focus to achieve. But the good news is that the reward is far greater, more fulfilling, and more substantial than you could ever possibly imagine.

> *"Men are anxious to improve their circumstances, but are*
> *unwilling to improve themselves, they therefore remain bound."*
> *—James Allen*

Ask yourself these important questions:

1. Is what you are doing with your life right now simply a substitute for what you know in your heart you *should* be doing?
2. What are you *not* doing with your life that you know deep down you should be doing and are fully capable of achieving?
3. What is it that you want to accomplish with your life?
4. What kind of person *are you*, and what kind of person do you *want to be*?
5. What *are* you doing with your dash, and what *should* you be doing with your dash?

It is completely up to you because, realize it or not, or even like it or not, *you* are in control of your own life and future. You have the power and ability to take your life in any direction you choose. You can completely alter the trajectory of your life and your future simply by *deciding* to do so, forming a plan, and taking action.

Know that you have the ability to live the life of your dreams, the life you are meant to live. It is entirely up to you. You can choose to step out above the average with faith and courage and live the life you have been given the talents, abilities, and gifts to live, or you can allow others and the random nature of life to choose for you. It is imperative for you to understand that we all have to implement our own deliberate plans for our lives or life will implement its own plan for us. Just know that you get what you choose in life, and the absence of an *intentional and deliberate* choice is, after all, still a choice. As Roman Emperor Marcus Aurelius said, "Our life is what our thoughts make it."

Did you know there is a mathematical equation for success in life? It is $V + A = S$, or Vision plus Action equals Success. This was shared with me many years ago through Zig Ziglar's work, and it literally changed my life. As Zig teaches, for you to have an *accurate* vision of what is possible for your life, you must first change the way you think. Because as Einstein pointed out, "The world as we have created it [meaning the world you have created for yourself] is a process of our thinking. It cannot be changed without changing our thinking." In other words, if you don't like the direction your life is moving in, then you have to take action and *do* something different, and this begins with changing what goes into your mind and the way you think. To quote Einstein again, "A problem cannot be solved by the same level of thinking at which it was created." In other words, if you never change the way you approach the challenges you face in your life, then you cannot expect things to be different, and nothing will ever change. Like a dog chasing his tail, you will just go round and round, confusing activity with accomplishment, growing older, and becoming more frustrated and disappointed with your life.

> *"There are two primary choices in life. We*
> *can accept conditions as they exist, or we can*
> *accept responsibility for changing them."*
> *–Denis Waitley*

Understand that it doesn't matter in the least *what* it is that you want to accomplish. This lesson could be applied to being a better parent or spouse, thus enjoying a more harmonious home life. It could be that you want to go back to school, get out of debt, achieve a promotion at work, start a new business, write a book, quit smoking, lose weight, get in shape, or anything else.

Everyone has something they want to accomplish and conditions in their life they wish to change or improve. For most, positive change is not possible because all they can see are the obstacles and challenges they face and, therefore, feel continually trapped and bound within the negative conditions of their lives.

You see, if you focus and dwell on your problems and on what you *believe* you lack, then all you will be able to see are the obstacles and challenges you face. But by changing the way you think, and thus changing your vision of what is possible for your life, you ignite a catalyst that sets in motion a chain of events that will absolutely change not just your life and your future, but also vastly improve the lives of those closest to you for generations to come.

It is vital to understand that when you change the way you *think*, this, over time and with sustained effort, gradually alters your view of yourself and what you believe is possible to accomplish in your life. When your *view* of yourself and what you believe is possible for your life changes, this gradually changes the overall *attitude* with which you approach everything you do, and when your attitude changes, this alters the expectations you have for your future.

Over time, as your *expectations* for your future change, this alters the manner in which you approach what you do in your day-to-day life, which ultimately, with sustained effort, changes your behavior. When your *behavior* changes, your performance changes. And when your *performance* changes, you completely transform your life and alter what is possible for your future.

This can be done in a positive direction that moves your life forward or in a negative direction that moves your life backwards... and the choice is yours!

Like laying building blocks, one atop another and weaving them together, this process, combined with patience, persistence, and consistent action, is the rock-solid foundation that places you on the path to accomplish any desire you have for your life. It all begins with altering and changing the way that you think and what goes into your mind. If you do not alter and improve your thought life and *intentionally* change the way you think, then nothing else you do will matter because nothing will ever change. There are no shortcuts here, and there is no "Plan B." Just know that unless we intentionally move our thoughts in a positive direction, then the changes in our lives will nearly always, by default, move in a negative direction. For most, these negative changes are subtle, so subtle that we do not even notice the change until we are trapped.

You see, we either have an attitude and vision that directs us closer to successful achievement, or we have an attitude and vision that directs us closer to complacency, apathy, and failure. Recognize that most who fail to accomplish the aims they have established for their lives, do so because they are unwilling to change, grow, and overcome even the smallest of challenges and obstacles they face. Know that every success begins with a correct and focused state of mind.

With determination and commitment, expand your vision of what is possible for you to accomplish with your life. With patience and persistence, begin right where you stand to renew your mind and increase the expectations you have for your future. Work diligently to build the faith and courage necessary to act upon your vision and follow through to the end. Decide *in advance* the direction of your life and know beyond any doubt *why* you make the choices and decisions that you do.

Take the time necessary to seek out quality mentors and humble yourself enough to listen to and follow their advice. Diligently work to eliminate pride from your life and remove any traces of a "victim" mentality from your thoughts and mind. Seek to understand why you think and believe as you do. Firmly establish your own belief system and know where these beliefs come from. Make every effort to identify what you value most in your life and know what is truly most important. Be willing to change and grow and always seek to learn where you need to improve. Do your best to better understand yourself, your weaknesses, and your vulnerabilities. Never allow past mistakes to define you or hold you back. Never allow the negative opinions of others to define you or limit your growth. Don't allow yourself to worry about what you think you lack or believe you do not possess. Strive to improve and strengthen every area of your life. Always focus on improving, strengthening, and protecting your character, continually and relentlessly moving forward.

With strength and courage, learn to work through the difficulties and challenges you face. Be determined to overcome and master your weaknesses. Work every day of your life to build your determination, inner strength, and your resolve. Learn to discipline yourself to stay focused on the most important areas of your life. Know that making an *intentional* and conscious decision about *who* you are, what you believe in, and the kind of person you will choose to be can be the single most important thing you will ever do in your life.

Take the first steps in action toward fulfilling your vision with absolute clarity of mind and purpose. Fully know in your heart the direction of your life and what you will do with your dash. Know that by changing the way you think, and thus changing your view of what is possible for your life and your future, you are taking hold of the keys to achieve any positive goal or vision you may have for your life.

Whatever goal you have for your life, persistence, patience, and discipline will get you there, but it is character and integrity that will *keep* you there.

The Big Idea

- Make intentional and deliberate decisions.
- Every success begins with a correct and focused state of mind.
- An excellent life is built intentionally.

Chapter 3

Esse Quam Videri: To Be Rather Than to Seem

HAVE you ever stopped at a state welcome center? It is kind of like a rest area along the interstate, but also has tourist information and details about the state you are visiting. I made a stop at such a place many years ago when I was moving to Charlotte and picked up a small brochure about the state of North Carolina. It had a bit of information about the history of the state, told the reader who the governor was, and provided other basic information. At the top of the brochure were the Latin words *Esse quam videri,* or translated, "To be rather than to seem." At the time, I paid little attention to them and just tossed the brochure in my car with the rest of my things, promptly forgetting about it.

Years later, while cleaning out a junk drawer, I rediscovered the brochure. As I read the brochure, the words struck me: *Esse quam videri… To be rather than to seem.* I had to pause and think a bit to grasp the full meaning of the words.

To me, "To be rather than to seem" is about actually *being* instead of *pretending* to be. It is about truly possessing a virtue instead of acting *as-if* or convincing yourself or others that you possess that virtue. It is about purposefully and deliberately living out certain values, a life of honesty and integrity, and pursuing a life of excellence with a pure heart and sincere motives. It is about seeking out what is right, regardless of the consequences and doing what is pleasing in the sight of God. As I continued to read the brochure, I learned that "To be rather than to seem" is the state motto of North Carolina, but I inherently knew it was much more than that.

For almost my entire working life, I was a salesman. I was taught that you do whatever it takes to make the sale. It's not that anyone ever came right out and said, "If you want to be successful, you should bend the truth to get ahead."… Oh, wait, sure they did! It was just part of the game. I don't mean to toss more Latin at you, but it was always *Caveat emptor,* or "buyer beware." The mantra signifying that deception is expected… To most in this environment, it was funny if they bought your line, and the prevailing attitude was to *seem* at all costs and *fake it 'til you make it.*

Was this unique to where I worked? No. Was this unique to the industry I was in? Absolutely not. It's simply the way business was and, sadly, still is done. Somehow the truth is *relative,* and the end always justifies the means. The prevailing attitude is that *everyone lies,* and if you are "strong enough" to be able to look someone else in the eye, muster up a dose of sincerity, and make someone else believe your lie because "it's just business," then somehow that is to be looked up to, admired, and rewarded. From the highest levels of business, religion, and government to our most important personal relationships, we somehow seem to find a way to rationalize the irrational and justify the unjustifiable.

So, is dishonest behavior and the temptation to deceive unique to today? Not at all, I would encourage you to study the lives of such ancients as Confucius or Roman Emperors Julius Caesar, Nero, Caligula, and Marcus Aurelius. Study the Psalms of King David and the writings of Homer, Plato, Aristotle, and Shakespeare. Look closely at the lives of Franklin Roosevelt, Winston Churchill, Dr. Martin Luther King, Jr., John F. Kennedy, and endless others. The trials, struggles, and temptations they faced were absolutely the same as today's, no different.

What *is* unique to our day is the sheer volume of the lapses we learn about, as well as the speed and multitude of different ways in which we learn about them. It seems that deception and dishonesty have become so common and pervasive that we have lost our capacity to be shocked by them. We almost expect to be lied to. We expect lousy service, and we are seldom surprised by dishonesty. It is no surprise at all when we learn of someone in a position of authority or responsibility who has been caught in an inappropriate relationship, cover-up, scandal, lie, or corruption.

It seems every day we are presented with yet another scandal, another deception, another investigation of those in power. In politics, as well as in business, normal and healthy competition has given way to an attitude of destroying the life and reputation of your opponent. If you can't win honestly, then cheat. If you can't beat 'em, bury 'em. The question becomes: Just how far can this go, and exactly where does this all end?

C.S. Lewis wrote in his book, *The Screwtape Letters*, "Courage is not simply one of the virtues but the form of every virtue at its testing point." Every human being since the fall of man has struggled with endless temptations, such as envy, jealousy, greed, intolerance, anger, and pride. The question is not *if* we will face these issues in our lives, the question is *how* we will face them. Will we face them with an attitude of, "Oh well, I'm only human" or "That's just how I am" and justify to ourselves why we aren't strong enough to rise above it? Or will we draw a line in the sands of our lives and take an honest assessment of who we are and what our lives are to be about?

After all, the very foundation of human decency,... the virtues of character, truth, and integrity, should *always* matter. You see, when we cease to be a society that values character, truth, and integrity, then we will ultimately cease to exist as decent and honorable people. And when we cease to exist as a decent and honorable people, what happens next, and precisely what do we do then?

So, we all have a choice to make. Will we choose to *seem* honest or actually *be* honest? How will the story of your life be told? What legacy will you choose to leave behind? What will your dash represent? Understand that this can be a conscious or an unconscious choice, but either way, it is a choice, and like it or not, it's one we all make.

The Big Idea

- Positive virtues are built deliberately.
- Character and integrity should always matter.
- Being honest is a choice.

Chapter 4
Aimless Distraction

If you aim at nothing, you will hit it every time.
–Zig Ziglar

TO be aimless means to lack direction or purpose, to drift, or to continually change. To be distracted is to have your attention diverted, have divided focus, or be unable to concentrate. This describes us all, at one time or another, but for far too many, our lives are perpetually aimless and far too easily distracted from what is most important.

The Bible tells us in Proverbs 21:5, "The plans of the diligent lead surely to abundance but everyone who is hasty comes only to poverty." We all desire abundance in our lives and not only in matters of money. We all want to enjoy abundant and meaningful relationships with our friends and family. We all want to enjoy lives filled with security and happiness. We want our careers to be meaningful and rewarding. We all want these things, yet so few ever seem to achieve what virtually every human being wants and even craves from their life. Why is that?

If you are married, you want to be loved wholly, deeply, and completely, and your spouse wants this type of love in return. If you have children, you want them to enjoy your complete acceptance and your total unconditional love. We all want to be able to fully immerse ourselves into any area of our lives that we feel passionate about, but this seldom actually happens. Why is this? Why is it that we merely dip our toe into areas of our lives where we should so willingly and eagerly dive in headfirst? What is it that keeps us from fully and completely committing ourselves to being the kind of spouse, parent, friend, employee, or student that we know we can be? What is it that keeps us from experiencing a deeply devoted, intimate, and personal relationship with God? What is it that blocks us from whole-heartedly participating in and enjoying what we know we can and should in our lives? **What is so important that it prevents us from what we know in our hearts we are fully capable of achieving?** The answer may surprise you because the answer is not much at all, nothing in particular, and absolutely nothing of significance.

There has never been a time in human history when there was more to occupy our attention and divide our focus than today. Because of this, we spend productive time at work distracted by trivial things when we should be laser-focused on our jobs. We spend our time at home parked in front of the television, computer, or cell phone, distracted by meaningless tasks, instead of concentrating on our families and their needs. We convince ourselves there will be time later or that we can do those things "someday," and we kick the can down the road to a someday that seldom if ever comes.

It is interesting that late in life, when asked about regrets, few people ever express regret over the things they did. In the vast majority of cases, the major regrets in life tend to be sifted down to the things we *didn't* do.

- Why didn't I take more vacations with the family?
- Why didn't I tell my spouse, children, or parents how much they mean to me and how much I love them?
- Why didn't I relax more?
- Why didn't I talk with God more and seek His wisdom?
- Why didn't I spend less time at work?
- Why didn't I start that business?
- Why didn't I give of myself more?
- And why was I so completely and aimlessly distracted from the things that were, ultimately, most important?

What do we need to do to be more productive at work or improve our relationships with our family, children, or friends? How do we stop, as Pastor Rick Warren says, "playing trivial pursuit with our lives" and begin to live lives filled with passion and wholeness? How do we learn to set aside all of the needless and seemingly never-ending distractions that bombard us day in and day out so that we can focus on what we deem most important in life?

Albert Schweitzer, the great psychologist and Nobel Prize winner, was once asked in an interview, "What is wrong with men today?" After a moment of thought, he responded by saying, "Men simply don't think." What Dr. Schweitzer points out is that most people tend to react to life instead of having a predetermined plan for their lives. Very few people live deliberate lives. We just go with the flow instead of living with a purpose, or we take it as it comes instead of having a premeditated and organized plan, one based on our needs, beliefs, and values.

I recall talking with the daughter of a friend of mine who had just moved back into her parents' home after separating from her husband. As she held her infant son, she told me story after story about the fiasco that was her marriage. She talked about how her husband had cheated on her and how often they fought. She talked about how he abused her and that he barely worked to support them. After listening to her sad story for nearly an hour, I asked her what she saw in him that made her think he was the one with whom she wanted to spend the rest of her life. To my surprise, she leaned back in her chair, balanced her infant son in her arms, and, as her face lit up, said, "Oh, I just loved the way he danced."

Why is it that so many of us make the major decisions in our lives based on *emotion* rather than *logic* or based on *convenience* rather than *reason*? To marry someone based on how that person makes you feel when they dance sounds crazy, but in reality, it is no different than a decision to make a career out of a particular job simply because a company had an opening and you were willing to fill it.

The fact is that very few of us ever take the time, effort, and energy to actually *plan* our lives. We focus on what is easy instead of what is right. We allow emotion to win over logic. We want it now instead of at its proper time. We want the path of least resistance instead of the road less traveled. We want to comfort ourselves in the short-term instead of pursuing what may be a long, hard road but to a much better place. We ultimately convince ourselves that achieving "success" and accumulating possessions is the key to happiness instead of understanding that true success lies in living a balanced life filled with purpose, peace, love, and wisdom.

Aimless distraction fades away when we focus on the areas of our lives that are most important and make a conscious decision about who we are, what we stand for, and what our lives are to be about. Aimlessness is replaced by focus when we know in our hearts we are on the right path, and distraction is replaced by discipline and purpose when we are pursuing a logical and predetermined plan for our lives.

The Big Idea

- Learn to focus on what is most important.
- Make important decisions based on logic, not emotion.
- Live life on purpose.

Chapter 5
Quiet Desperation

Quietly desperate so no one will see, we
think we can fool them all.
Puttin' on a grin, tough pain is within,
we certainly miss the call.

WHAT does it mean to be desperate? It could be best described as a state of despair, typically one that results in rash, reckless, or extreme behavior.

"Quiet desperation" means living each day with a tiny dose of anxiety and a constant, nagging feeling of dread. It is waking up each morning with that little knot in your gut that won't go away or allow you to ever completely relax.

To the outside world, you may give the impression that life couldn't possibly be better, but the truth is that you're continually yet quietly afraid or desperate about what might be coming around the corner.

- Am I going to be caught in the lie I told?
- Am I going to be able to pay my mortgage?
- Am I going to lose my job?
- Am I going to be able to afford to send my kids to college?
- Am I going to be able to retire?
- Am I going to be *found out?*

And on and on and on…

It is when we incrementally and systematically imprison ourselves to such things as an overload of debt, an entanglement of lies, destructive or inappropriate relationships, that we dig a hole for ourselves, one in which we are continuously trying to find a way out of. When our hearts and minds are filled with worry, fear, anxiety, jealousy, and envy, our focus is on staying one step ahead of these negative aspects of our lives; and this prevents us from focusing on what is most important.

I recall a television commercial that spoke to this issue. It showed a tall, tanned, well-dressed man describing the trappings of his seemingly successful life. He looks straight at the camera and says, "I have a five-bedroom house on a golf course. I am a member of the country club. I have two brand new cars." Then he asks the viewers the question, "How do I do it?" He then answers, "I'm in debt up to my eyeballs." Then with a wide grin, he begs, "Somebody help me."

The humorist Will Rogers once observed, "We spend money we don't have, to buy things we don't need, to impress people we don't even know." No matter what trappings of "success" we are able to display, we have to ask ourselves what the real value is if we are secretly anxious about paying the bills, quietly worried about our relationships, or desperate about life in general. This leaves little room for us to grow or have the mental freedom required to live up to our full potential. After all, how can a man ever be truly free if he is a prisoner, even if it's a self-imposed prison?

Henry David Thoreau wrote about his personal experience after spending two years alone in a cabin deep in the wilderness at Walden Pond in Massachusetts. These years inspired him to write, "Most men lead lives of quiet desperation and go to the grave with the song still in them." Thoreau went on to say, "I went to the woods because I wished to live deliberately, to front only the essential facts of life, and see if I could not learn what it had to teach, and not, when I came to die, discover that I had not lived…"

Another way to say it is that Thoreau put himself in "time out." It is difficult to know who we truly are if we are continually trying to be someone else or find ourselves focused on living up to what we think others expect from us.

When we live a life outside of our means, are untruthful, have secrets or inappropriate relationships, we invite a multitude of negative consequences into our lives, including anxiety, stress, anger, and resentment. When these fill our lives, we find ourselves continually reacting to the negative situations we have created and struggle to stay in pace with life, let alone one step ahead.

There are always lessons to be learned, and we need to be willing to take the time to learn them *and* to understand them. Never allow yourself to focus on how you think your life compares to others. Always strive to be content with what you have but continually seek to build and strengthen your character. Learn to humble yourself. Be willing to admit when you are wrong. Allow yourself to be vulnerable and seek the help and guidance of others. Seek God's wisdom and strive to learn from your own challenges and mistakes, as well as those of others. Be diligent in understanding there are *seasons of life* and with dedicated effort and patience, know that everything will come in its proper time.

When we are honest in our dealings with ourselves and others, we free our minds, which allows us to gain a better perspective; only then can we truly focus on the most important areas of life. Know that living a life of truth, honesty, integrity, and positive character is the key to a life of freedom; for when we free our minds, it is only then that we can be truly free.

The Big Idea

- Freedom begins with freeing our minds.
- Never compare your life to others.
- Truth really does set us free.

Chapter 6
Self-Awareness and Self-Observation

"Everyone thinks of changing the world,
but no one thinks of changing himself."
–Leo Tolstoy

Observe the Animal

IN a science class that I took long ago, the instructor brought a small brown rabbit into the classroom. The rabbit sat in a wire cage, which was surrounded by a bag of food, a container of water, bedding, hay, medical supplies, and various other items which rabbits might need.

Our assignment was to, as a class, determine what the rabbit would require *first*. On the board at the front of the classroom was a list of a dozen or so different tasks, which seemed to be obvious choices. As the instructor went around the room, we all called out what we thought was the correct answer to what the rabbit would need *first*.

"Feed it," one student called out. "Give it water," shouted another. Other students provided answers, such as clip its nails, let it exercise, clean its cage, and so on. As each logical task from the list was called out, the instructor would say "no" and mark it off of the board. We quickly moved through all of the choices, with the exception of one: observe the animal.

Observe the animal…?

"Are you kidding," we thought. "That can't be right." We could all see the rabbit when we walked into the room, and besides, "Just because that is what we *did* first, that doesn't mean that's what the rabbit *needed* first," we argued. Feeling tricked, we challenged the instructor.

"How could observing the rabbit be more important than giving it food or water?" one student asked.

"It has plenty of food and water," the instructor answered. And with that, she pointed out there is much more to "observing" something than simply seeing it or looking at it. She went on to teach us that the only way to truly know and understand what the rabbit would need *first* was to look well past the superficial and the obvious and study each and every area of the rabbit's life in specific detail.

What does it mean to observe? Most would say it means to watch carefully and with diligence or to study with the intent to gain knowledge. In this case, it meant to look well beyond the surface level and closely examine each and every area of the rabbit's life so that we could truly understand what the animal needed. This is the first and most important fundamental step to having true insight about any animal, especially ourselves.

If you really do want an excellent life, self-awareness and self-observation are where it all begins, and are absolute musts for true personal growth in all areas of our lives. Know that to achieve true and meaningful change in our lives, we must first become a student of *ourselves*. Simply put, it is only through fully understanding how we got to where we are that we can know what it will take to get to where we want to be.

Understand that self-awareness can be a challenging and life-changing exercise, that requires complete and total honesty with the one person who is usually most difficult for us to be honest with and the one we attempt to deceive the most... ourselves.

The "Wheel of Life"

One of the greatest advantages I have had in my life was to be closely mentored and coached via audio by an incredibly gifted and wise teacher named Zig Ziglar. I got to know Zig's teachings at a very young age and have had the benefit of his knowledge, insight, and wisdom without fail for over forty years. I can honestly say that every time I have needed the benefit of such a wise teacher, he was there for me, whispering in my ear. Though I only met him in person once, there is no doubt that Zig Ziglar has been one of the most important and impactful mentors in my life.

I am eternally thankful that I have been able, through technology, to sit with Zig for endless hours while he spoke with me about how to stay positive in such a negative world and the importance of self-motivation and self-discipline. Thanks to his remarkable ability to make each listener feel as if he is speaking directly to them, I was able to build the confidence and courage I needed to follow in his footsteps and become a salesman, a business owner, and ultimately, a leader in my profession.

Hardly a day goes by that I don't have an issue come up that reminds me of something Zig taught me about life, faith, or family. I count among the many blessings of my life that I have been fortunate enough to become friends with Zig's only son, Tom, and that I can, in some small way, assist in carrying out the legacy his father started so long ago.

Among the most meaningful insights I learned from Zig was how important it is to continually observe and examine ourselves. He understood and taught that it is impossible to live an excellent life without meaningful growth through self-awareness, and the way he taught about self-awareness was through something he called "The Wheel of Life." Indeed, the Wheel of Life was Zig's unique construct for teaching us all how to *observe the animal.*

Through the Wheel of Life, Zig divided life into seven specific and individual areas, those being Family, Personal (which includes friends), Career, Physical, Financial, Spiritual, and Mental. As hard as I have tried, I cannot come up with an area of life that is not covered by one of these seven.

The genius of what Zig Ziglar taught is that true success is found in living a *balanced life*. Without balance in our lives, too much emphasis is placed on one or two areas to the exclusion of the others. After all, what good does it do any of us to have a successful career if our physical health is neglected and suffers because of it? Or how can anyone be considered truly successful if we have a lot of money and yet spend life as a stranger to our own family? Leading a life without the closeness of family, friends, or quality relationships is a shallow and empty existence, which no one could rightfully describe as successful. Likewise, what kind of life would it be to have strong relationships or a meaningful spiritual life while we dishonor ourselves, God, and our families because we can't live up to our obligations or pay our bills?

To give us a visual to work with, Zig formed the seven areas into a wheel, giving each of the areas a place as a "spoke" in the wheel as shown below:

As you can see, beside each of the seven areas are the numbers 1 through 10 with 1 being at the center of the wheel and 10 being at the outside. What Zig asks us to do is to examine ourselves through the Wheel of Life and give ourselves an honest grade with 1 being poor and 10 being excellent. The objective of assessing each of the seven areas is to become aware of those areas in our lives where we are excelling, as well as to understand the areas in which we are lacking, with the ultimate goal of achieving balance in our lives. Understand that the objective is to achieve improvement and *balance* and not *perfection*.

The reason a wheel is such an excellent visual is that it is easy for us to see if or when we have a "flat tire" in areas of our lives that need to be fixed. If we have a 7, 8, or 9 in some areas and a 2, 3, or 4 in others, it's not difficult to understand how our lives could be more productive and meaningful if we take the time necessary to examine with absolute honesty how we can improve in the areas where we are lacking.

Understand that nothing in life remains still for very long. Things are either moving forward or backward. You are either moving closer to or further from where you want to be, and it is surprising how quickly we can slide backward and not even realize it.

Be aware that self-improvement and moving forward in life is a constant and never-ending battle between pride and humility. When we make obvious strides forward, we tend to become prideful, and when we go through trials, we learn what it feels like to be humble… and the process starts all over again.

The key is to be aware of and monitor your weaknesses, your progress, and your growth. Learn to recognize what circumstances in your life tend to cause you to digress and what it takes for you to experience steady progress. Continually refine your thought life and introduce yourself to new challenges that will excite and motivate you. Find ways to limit or even cast aside from your life anything that is negative, causes temptation, or could cause you to stumble.

One thing that will be very helpful is to fill out Zig's Wheel of Life and take note of the results. Then have your spouse or someone who knows you best fill it out with you in mind. Make note of and discuss the differences. This is important because you will need to know just how honest you are being with yourself. After comparing, adjust each of the seven areas with the average of the two different results.

Understand that this is designed to be an ongoing process and not a "one and done."... To achieve maximum benefit, complete the Wheel of Life exercise at the beginning of each month, and make note of any changes. This is vital so you can continually keep all seven areas top of mind and drive them deep into your subconscious, to a point where you can easily recognize any time there is the potential to grow and learn. This has proven particularly powerful for me in providing an ongoing way to focus on and improve every area of my life. Continual focus on all seven areas has also allowed me to be mindful of anything that could cause me to digress and, thus, quickly make necessary changes and adjustments.

Slowly, and over time you will discover that you are becoming more selective about how you spend your time and where you direct your energies. As you continue to grow, you will find yourself ready to take on new challenges and new opportunities, not to mention enjoy the feeling of personal empowerment and satisfaction that certainly follows.

Over time, with patience, persistence, and focus, you will achieve steady progress in every area of your life and move ever closer to achieving the necessary balance you seek. As you progress, you will find that you are experiencing less stress and a welcomed calmness and resilience. As a result, you may notice that you have become much more focused, and self-aware and experience a much higher level of productivity.

It is important to be aware that this process is not in any way about striving for perfection or trying to achieve a "10" in any specific area, much less in all seven. It's simply not possible or even practical to believe that we can somehow achieve and maintain a perfect level of balance in a life that is always changing and evolving. For this reason, we must be willing to allow for the ebb and flow of life and realize that continual change and re-balancing is predictable and normal.

We should always be mindful of the ever-changing seasons of life and accept that within these seasons, some areas of our lives will, for a time, require more focus and attention than others. The goal is simply to identify and recognize the most important priorities in life within any given season, and therefore strive to achieve the correct balance of the seven different areas... and only *you* can determine what that is for your life.

In my view, the correct approach is to routinely balance and re-balance as the seasons of life change. Never allow any one area to lag too far behind the others or be ignored. All seven areas of our lives are vital to achieving a life of peace, prosperity, and excellence. The key is to be aware of your priorities and of where the major focus of your energy and attention should be at any given time so you can be fully engaged on the most important tasks at hand. This means that when you are at work, it is time to be focused on work. When it is time for family or friends, learn to relax so you can be fully focused on family and friends, and so on. If you are married, I highly recommend implementing this with your spouse so that the most important areas and events of your lives can be discussed in detail and planned together. When possible, your children should also be included, even at young ages. This way, they will develop a full understanding of the larger pictures of their lives and are mentored and taught to realize the importance of achieving balance within their lives as well.

Be mindful that as you grow and learn and your ability to focus on each independent area of your life evolves and improves, you will slowly discover more about yourself and begin to take on a new poise, confidence, and inner strength. As time progresses and as you work through the Wheel of Life, you will find that you are becoming much more purposeful in your approach to each area of your life and will gradually, over time, develop a new calmness and inner peace.

As you progress, your perspective of the Wheel of Life will slowly evolve and change as you grow. You will gradually discover at some point that the Wheel will, in effect, invert in your own heart and mind, becoming something much different and much more powerful. As you grow, your focus will begin to change from one that is directed inward, on yourself and your own goals, wishes, and desires, to one that is much more outwardly directed and more *selfless*.

At some point in this process, you will find yourself focusing more on others in your life and on how you can help them grow and improve. You will slowly begin to take on a larger view of life with an understanding that life is not about *you* and what you want; rather, it is understanding that an excellent life is about helping and improving the lives of others and being a blessing to those around you.

With continued growth and refinement, you will ultimately replace *yourself* as the "center" of your life, and in its place, you will begin to focus more on God. As you grow and progress, He will ultimately become your rock and the foundation on which everything in your life is built.

During this journey, at the point when you fully and completely put your focus on God and His wishes for your life instead of on yourself, the Wheel of Life will undoubtedly alter and change to this:

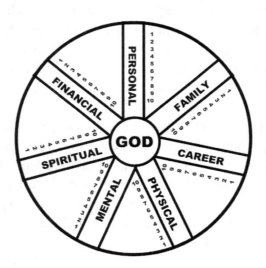

Take notice that the numbers have changed their position on the wheel in that 1 (or poor) is now at the outside of the wheel and 10 (or excellent) is closest to the center, which is closest to God. Know that as we learn to focus on God and His will—instead of merely our own—we naturally grow in all areas of our lives as we grow closer to Him. We begin to understand that life is not about achieving self-serving goals and building monuments to ourselves but about worshiping God and building our character to best suit His purpose for our lives.

As we learn to set aside our own wants, wishes, and desires and earnestly seek to understand God's will, we grow ever closer to Him. Through this process, we naturally learn how to become a better parent to our children. We become a better spouse and friend and develop deeper, more intimate personal relationships. We learn to put our careers in the proper perspective, and with time, we become a better steward of His money. As we continue to grow, we develop a better understanding of the importance of taking care of our physical bodies and continually seek to improve our knowledge and our wisdom.

We grow in these areas of our lives because we have learned to completely trust God and are focused on His wishes and His will. Because of this, our faith is increased to a point where we can easily and confidently turn every area of our lives over to Him, no longer doing these things for ourselves, rather doing them for God, knowing He is in control.

With God in control and at the center of our lives and as we surrender ourselves to Him, we can more easily set aside our daily worries, concerns, and fears. We are better able to deal with bouts of pride and take on a humbler view of ourselves, which leads to a natural and unwavering balance. With God as our focus and at the center of our lives, we gradually develop an unshakeable faith because our lives are built on an unshakeable foundation that will not be eroded.

With diligence, *observe the animal* within. Take the time necessary to truly know yourself in an intimate and honest way. Learn your strengths, as well as your weaknesses and vulnerabilities. Make it a priority to learn what influences you to act and react the way you do. Understand that true change can only happen in life **after** we diligently observe and truly understand, not merely the world around us, but ultimately, *ourselves*.

Understand that we will all face tests and trials in our lives; no one is ever exempt from that. Know that if we place anything at the center of our lives except God, when those trials come, we may not have enough strength to carry us through. Understand that any and all areas of our lives can be taken away from us, and if we place anything at the center of our lives to the exclusion of God and make it our foundation, we are then made vulnerable, thus making stability and balance impossible.

Know that it is only through observing, studying, and understanding *ourselves* that we are able to make the necessary changes in our lives to predictably grow and progress. You will find that this process is essential in helping you achieve what we all require to live a happy, fulfilled, and excellent life… balance.

The Big Idea

- Be ever mindful of the changing seasons of life.
- To achieve an excellent life, you must achieve *balance*.
- Continual self-awareness and self-observation are the key to balance.

Chapter 7
Why We Struggle

"The same hammer that breaks glass also forges steel."
—Russian Proverb

WHEN I was growing up, my family would sometimes stay for a week or so each summer at a relative's cabin in the Blue Ridge Mountains in northern Georgia. It was a very rustic place, built on a steep kudzu-covered hill overlooking the flowing white rapids of the Tallulah River.

This was a kid's paradise. We floated down the river's rapids in inner tubes, fished for rainbow trout, had bonfires, and went on endless hikes through the deep woods that surrounded the red cedar cabin. It was on such a hike that we came across a butterfly chrysalis. I had seen many of these before, but this was unique because the caterpillar had already turned into a butterfly and was almost finished with its struggle to escape the tight confines of its chrysalis.

We just stood there in silent amazement as the butterfly completed its final battle for freedom and then majestically hung on the bottom side of the chrysalis in a brilliant and breathtaking pose.

As we watched, the butterfly seemed to struggle with its wings. In an attempt to help the butterfly, my father took a small twig and placed it against its tiny legs, and it cautiously crawled onto the twig. My father then carefully placed the butterfly on the top side of a small tree limb. Still struggling, the butterfly twitched and quivered, then ever so slowly attempted to raise its wings. As it did, the butterfly lost its balance and awkwardly rolled off of the limb and tumbled to the ground below.

It lay on the ground, frantically twitching its wings and trying to regain its balance, but to no avail. More than a little disappointed, we could only wonder what was up with our defective butterfly. It wasn't until many years later that I understood my father's act of "helping" the butterfly actually caused it to fail to achieve its *purpose*.

You see, it was necessary for the butterfly to struggle because the very act of the struggle makes the butterfly stronger. As it struggles, blood and fluid are pumped into the wings, giving them the necessary strength to fly. The butterfly *cannot* be fully transformed into what it is intended to become until it has fully completed its struggle. And so it is with us all. There has never been a human being that has not faced trials, struggles, and difficult times in their life. Know that it is through the many struggles of life that the limits of our future potential are increased and expanded. Without struggles, we cannot grow; without trials, we digress; without resistance, we grow weak; without challenges, we are complacent and, thus, ill-prepared when the inevitable storms of life come our way.

Think about the lives of Abraham Lincoln, Winston Churchill, Helen Keller, and Martin Luther King, Jr. and know that *no one* can live up to their full potential without trials and struggles. No great person ever became great without *first* learning what it feels like to struggle to overcome what can seem to be overwhelming obstacles.

Franklin Roosevelt's battle with polio not only gave him the compassion and humility it took to lead America out of the Great Depression, but also the determination and iron-like fortitude it took to lead the free world through the darkest days of World War II. Nelson Mandela spent twenty-seven years as a political prisoner in South Africa, enduring horrible and cruel conditions, and yet, went on to become president of the very nation that had imprisoned him. And after his ship was cut in half by a Japanese destroyer, a young naval lieutenant named John F. Kennedy was forever changed as he learned courage and leadership in the waters of the Solomon Islands.

> *"Strength does not come from physical capacity.*
> *It comes from an indomitable will."*
> —*Mahatma Gandhi*

It is simply part of the human condition that we cannot grow or become stronger unless we face difficulties or *resistance* in our lives and work to overcome them. We can only grow stronger when the limits of our strength of will and resolve are tested. Each one of us learns *how* to be strong, and we become increasingly stronger, by facing increasingly difficult tests and challenges in our lives. If we are in any way sheltered or protected from the challenges and trials of life, when true adversity comes, we will be fragile, weak, and ill-prepared.

Consider those who were raised during the Great Depression. The suffering that transpired during this extremely difficult time affected nearly every man, woman, and child. Almost no one was untouched by the negative effects of an economy that had quite literally collapsed. The events of this time in our history can be viewed in many different ways, but there can be no argument about the fact that the trials and sufferings that took place during the Great Depression left an indelible mark on everyone who lived through it. With the possible exception of the Civil War and the Revolutionary War years, the struggles this particular group of Americans dealt with on a daily basis are all but unknown to other generations. Due to the many trials of the Great Depression, this generation of Americans learned hard and valuable lessons, which were completely foreign to their parents or grandparents. They developed an intimate knowledge of what it means to sacrifice. They learned what it means to work hard and for little in return. They learned firsthand what it means to live day-to-day, with no knowledge of what the future holds. They intimately experienced what it means to be hungry and to make unimaginable sacrifices for those they love. As the Depression dragged on year after year, they learned how to adapt and adjust. They learned to build hope where seemingly none existed. They learned to work together through the growing uncertainty and to suffer through even the most difficult and challenging of times.

This generation was hardened by their experiences; they were honed by their challenges, and as a result, they were extremely tough in mind, body, and spirit. They developed an unimaginable resolve, a high level of discipline, an absolute strength of will, and a true depth of character. It is because of the duration of the Depression, which lasted over ten years, that they learned to persist in their survival. The net result was that they were uniquely prepared for the much larger and unimaginable challenge ahead... World War II.

> *"This generation of Americans has a rendezvous with destiny."*
> *–Franklin Roosevelt*

I would argue that if it were not for the trials and lessons learned by this generation during the complex difficulties of the Great Depression, America would have been woefully ill-prepared for what it took to stand up against the new and even larger trials they faced. The sacrifices our nation endured to defeat Nazi Germany and the Empire of Japan were in many ways second nature to this generation of men and women. It is because of the obstacles from their past that they were able to be transformed into the kind of people it took to overcome and defeat the greatest challenge in human history and, quite literally, to save the entire world from an unimaginable and unrelenting evil.

Understand that within every struggle lies the foundation of future achievement and growth in our lives. When life gets tough—and it will— the trials we face are those we are meant to go through *and* to overcome. When the hammer of harsh circumstances comes down in our lives, if we are fragile, we will break like glass. But if we demonstrate faith and meet adversity head-on, we will be forged into something even stronger and much more substantial. Just as with the butterfly, we face challenges and struggles in our lives so that we can one day spread our wings and be transformed into the person we were created to be, living up to our true and full potential. We have no way of knowing what lies ahead in our lives. Just know that the many trials of life are inevitable, so learn to press on through the difficult times and overcome them with honor, dignity, courage, and integrity.

Know that it is during difficult times that we learn humility and build character and wisdom. It is when life challenges us the most that we can overcome envy, greed, and jealousy. It is when we think we cannot continue that we look deep within ourselves and develop the invaluable habits of patience and persistence. It is when life hits us the hardest that we build fortitude and learn to overcome false pride and self-pity. It is not until we have overcome what we once thought we could not that we experience the overwhelming feeling of confident satisfaction that can *only* come from facing and overcoming our deepest insecurities and fears. It is when we are fully immersed in an overwhelming trial that we *finally* forget ourselves and develop compassion, empathy, and a giving heart. It can often be at our lowest point that we turn to God, and through *Him*, the foundation of our faith and character is then made firm.

No one ever led an excellent life without learning in their gut through the trials they face *how* to persist and move forward, even when we think we have no strength left. It is in the midst of our trials that we learn to trust God completely and realize it is *because* we struggle that we can ultimately become forged into someone who is able to achieve the absolute greatest of accomplishments.

Know this: no one can ever be greater than the mountains they have not climbed. For things to change in your life, *you* need to change. Never yield control of your life and the fate of your future to the obstacles and challenges that you face. Never wish for life to be easier; rather, strive to be stronger. Do not ask for fewer problems; work to improve your skills. Do not plead for fewer challenges, but pray for wisdom, strength, and understanding.

Adversity and tragedy are a part of life, and they can rip you apart or they can galvanize you and make you stronger. Learn to take on a larger view of life's challenges and know that they are not meant to hold you back or limit your future, but to make you stronger and to unleash your full potential. Look deep within yourself and learn to run *toward* your obstacles and fears and face life's trials standing up, running full speed. Know that the trials and adversity we all face in life are beaten back and overcome by standing up to them with faith, wisdom, and courage. Live every day of your life knowing that facing life's challenges will forge you into a person of confidence, strength, and persistence, and no excuses and no regrets.

I challenge you to pass down to your children and grandchildren a legacy of faith, courage, honesty, and integrity. Pass down to them a life of fortitude and strong will, of wisdom, and of victory. Do this, and the blood of life will be pumped into you *and* into those closest to you so that for generations to come, will be able to soar with heads held high, having done as God intended, one day hearing these words from God Himself: "Well done, my good and faithful servant."

The Big idea

- You were created for a purpose.
- Your struggles exist to give you the strength necessary to achieve your purpose.
- Persist and never give up.

Chapter 8
What Is Love?

DOES the word *love* make you think about anyone or anything specific? If you are married or have children, does this word prompt you to think about your spouse or children and how much they mean to you.

One of my favorite quotes about love is from author Susan Forward who wrote, "Love is a verb, not a noun. It is active. Love is not just feelings of passion and romance. It is behavior."

A quick internet search finds countless definitions of love, including "a feeling of strong or constant affection for someone or something." Or "an intense feeling of deep emotions." In our society and language, it can be said that we love people, we love our pets, or we can love things or even ideals, but for our current purposes, we will focus on loving other people.

Deep and powerful emotions may accompany love, but is love merely about how we *feel*, or is there a deeper and more meaningful aspect of love, which we should explore and seek to better understand?

Know that if you truly want an excellent life, this cannot be achieved without having close and loving relationships in your life. It is undeniable that each and every one of us was built to love and to be loved.

I believe there is a subtle but very substantial difference in the quality of our lives based on how we view love. If our focus is mainly on what we *receive* from those we love, then when we, in our own assessments, do not receive what we think we are entitled to or receive it in ways we don't want or expect, then love for us tends to be shallow and disappointing. On the other hand, if our focus is on what we *give* to those we love, then love becomes fulfilling, satisfying, and deeply rewarding.

It is important to point out that our closest relationships should never be about what we *receive* from those in our lives who we profess to love. How we give or choose to display our love for others should never, in any way be about performance or what they can *do* for us. To love someone but to have selfish or insincere motives in your heart is not love at all but actually a form of manipulation, which can be quite destructive. Conversely, when we have pure and sincere motives, we grow closer to those in our lives who are most important to us. Know that with time, developing a heart of love builds, shapes, and adds depth to our character in ways otherwise not imaginable or even thought to be possible.

"Love does not dominate, it cultivates."
–Johann Wolfgang von Goethe

Throughout the Bible, in both the Old and New Testaments, we are instructed in how we are to love one another. In fact, there are more than 500 verses of Scripture that speak about the many different kinds of love.

My favorite definition for how we are to love one another is from the Biblical Counseling Foundation, which says love is "a purposeful commitment to sacrificial action for another." Let's examine this for a minute. This tells us that the true intention of love is for it to be "a purposeful commitment."

What exactly is a purposeful commitment? The use of the word *purposeful* in this context means intentional and deliberate; it is a choice and not random or by chance. It is premeditated, carefully thought out, preplanned, or literally, "on purpose."

The word *commitment* means that we are completely dedicated to someone, or it is a promise that we make, such as in a marriage vow. So, a "purposeful commitment" means that we *deliberately choose to dedicate ourselves to someone.* Or said another way, love is a *choice*, and we intentionally and deliberately choose to dedicate ourselves to others.

The term *sacrificial action* means just that. When we truly love someone and have dedicated ourselves to them, we are willing to do anything we can for them, and in the process, make what can often be viewed as tremendous sacrifices. We sacrifice our time, energy, money, health, or in some cases, our very lives. Why? *Because we love them.*

Notice that this definition of love does not say or even suggest that love is an emotional state. Rather, love is a state of action, which is a choice or something we *do*, not something we merely *feel*. The Bible tells us in 1 John 3:18 (NLT), "Dear children, let's not merely say that we love each other. Let us show the truth by our actions." Thus, we can choose to love someone, or we can choose to *not* love someone, and too often, we tend to choose one way or another based on our fleeting emotions or trivial aspects of our experiences with those in our lives.

I always find it interesting when someone says that they have "fallen out of love" with someone. What they are actually saying is they have *decided* to not love, having made a decision or *choice* (consciously or not) to harden their emotions toward someone and, therefore, no longer love them. We allow our love for others to slip away because we slowly and incrementally develop different interests or priorities and, by default, choose to no longer make the relationship a priority in our lives.

> *"Love is not affectionate feeling, but a steady wish for the loved person's ultimate good as far as it can be obtained."*
> –C.S. Lewis

Let me put this on a personal level. I love my wife! I mean, I really love her, and I love her with everything that I am and everything that is within me. Because I love her so deeply and completely, I would do almost anything for her, even give up my own life for her. Now, do I enjoy the things she does for me and the things we do together? Yes, of course. Do I like that she is beautiful? Absolutely. Do I appreciate that she is very intelligent and how sweet and kind she is? You bet. There are endless things about her that make me want to *be* with her and that make me want her to be a part of my life, but none of these are the reason I love her. You see, all of the things I mentioned that I enjoy, like, or appreciate about her can, and will, over the years fade or even go away completely, but my love for her will never fade.

You see, I choose to love her because we have the same beliefs and value system. I choose to love her because we have the same view of life. I choose to love her because her priorities are in the right place. And I am very grateful because she chooses to love me in return, for better or for worse.

The hard fact is that our most important relationship decisions are too often based on short-term and trivial things—such as looks, money, social status, or just having fun—when they should be based on character, values, and common beliefs. As William Shakespeare put it in *A Midsummer's Night Dream*, "Love looks not with the eyes but with the mind."

Let's talk about what love *is* and *is not*, for I believe it's essential to know the difference.

For most of us, love is strictly about the emotional feeling we have when we are *in love*. There is an amazing amount of depth that can be achieved in our lives *if* and *when* we truly understand love in the deepest possible sense.

I really like the words from 1 Corinthians 13:4–7 (NLT) which say, "Love is patient and kind. Love is not jealous or boastful or proud or rude. It does not demand its own way. It is not irritable, and it keeps no record of being wronged. It does not rejoice about injustice but rejoices whenever the truth wins out. Love never gives up, never loses faith, is always hopeful, and endures through every circumstance."

Let's take a close look at this verse and address each facet of love that it points out.

Love is patient. Being patient in love or with love is simply accepting that the people in our lives are human and, therefore, have flaws. To love someone is to accept all the imperfections they carry as just part of what we love about them. Because of our love, we are able to look past their imperfections without complaint or anger. I am certainly far from perfect, and my wife is obviously the most patient human being on the planet because she loves me for who I am and with all of my flaws, which I have no doubt requires, at times, a lot of patience.

During the writing of this book, my wife was diagnosed with breast cancer. Ironically, she found out she had cancer just a day or so after I had completed writing the chapter titled "Why We Struggle." When she told me she had cancer, all I could do was to express my genuine love for her and accept what she was going to face with love, support, gentleness, and patience. I can honestly say that going through that experience, which lasted about eighteen months, brought us much closer together and left us with more love for each other than I believe either of us had ever experienced or even thought possible.

Love is kind. This is about all the little things. The small loving gestures, the impromptu hugs, the little *I love yous*, the small notes, holding the door open, supportive comments, running errands, and doing small favors. Showing kindness is simply being gentle and caring with love.

Love is not jealous. When we love someone, their successes are our successes, and there should never be any rivalry or resentment. Always speak well of those you love and build them up. Breathe life into all they do and all they can be. Let those whom you love know just how much you believe in them. Be happy for their accomplishments and always be supportive.

Love is not boastful. Who wants to be with someone who brags all the time? The attitude of "I'm all that" or actions that make those in our lives believe that we look down on them or that we are in some way superior to them have no place in a true, loving relationship.

Love is not proud. Pride is just plain destructive. To have an over-inflated opinion of ourselves or to draw an undue amount of pleasure from our own achievements does not and cannot foster love in any relationship and only leads to conflict or even destruction. Unchecked pride can be the most damaging force on earth.

Love is not rude. Rudeness gets old quickly. Nobody wants to be around someone who is rude. Enough said!

Love does not demand its own way. I will go even further. Love is not demanding at all, and important decisions should always be made together with everyone's best interest in mind.

Love is not irritable. Let's face it; we can all be irritable. But it should be the rare exception, and if you have been irritable with anyone, apologize sincerely, learn from the experience, and move on.

Love keeps no record of being wronged. One of the many things I admire and appreciate about my wife is that she has a very short memory regarding the shortcomings of others. No one wants to be continually held accountable for issues and mistakes they've made in the past. If someone does something wrong, once they have apologized sincerely for it, the matter should be dropped, and not dwelled upon.

Love does not rejoice about injustice but rejoices when the truth wins out. Always strive to be on the side of truth and develop a strong sense of justice. Stand up for those you love and come to their defense when necessary. Learn to recognize injustice. Choose to be a protector and defender of those who cannot defend themselves. Always seek the truth in every situation and learn to live out every circumstance in life with honor and integrity. Make it a point to be a quality mentor in this area, and, by your example, help those around you develop a heart for helping the weak and most vulnerable among us.

Love never gives up, never loses faith. Giving up and losing faith go hand in hand. One of my favorite quotes is from Winston Churchill who said, "If you are going through hell, keep going." Let's face it, sometimes in the midst of a test or trial, we will feel like throwing our hands in the air and quitting. Just understand the test or trial for what it is—temporary. It will end, and you and your relationships will be better and stronger because you stayed strong and remained deliberate and steadfast in your faith, as well as in your love for each other.

Love is always hopeful and endures through every circumstance. With love, we have a strong and confident expectation that no matter what we face, we can—and will—prevail and our love will endure. And indeed, with faith, hope, and love, we will grow stronger through every circumstance.

I believe the three most powerful words uttered from the lips of humankind are "I love you," and for this reason, Gandhi once said, "Love is the law of life." To me, this points out that a life without expressing and receiving love is no life at all, and to live our lives without consistently and passionately giving ourselves to others can never be described as an excellent life or a life well-lived. You see, it is simply against our nature as human beings to truly love without displaying that love through earnestly giving ourselves to others.

Loving one another and developing a heart of love are meant to be the cornerstone and the very foundation of our lives here on earth. Love should be demonstrated not merely with our words, but also by our continuous actions and interactions with one another. In its simplest and most basic form, and as Forrest Gump might have said, "Love is as love does."

Know that a successful and excellent life is simply unachievable without having close, loving, and meaningful relationships in our lives. Those closest to us need to know how we feel about them. Never be shy about telling others how much you love them, what they mean to you, and how proud you are of them.

There is nothing in this life more important than earnestly and completely expressing our love for others. Do this, and your life will be richer, fuller, and more rewarding than you could ever imagine. For when you learn to love unselfishly, you learn the eternal secret of a life fully lived.

The Big Idea

- Love is a purposeful commitment to sacrificial action for another.
- Love should never be about what we *receive* from others.
- An excellent life is unachievable without close and loving relationships.

Chapter 9
Guard Your Mind: Garbage in, Garbage Out

"Do not conform to the pattern of this world, but be transformed by the renewing of your mind..."
—Romans 12:2, NIV

JERRY and Donna have been married for twelve years and have two children—Jake, eight, and Caroline, six. They all look forward to Christmas; it is a special time of year for each of them for many reasons, but for Caroline, this particular Christmas was about *Santa* bringing her very own stereo. She loves music, and her big brother was not so willing to share with his little sister.

On Christmas Eve, Caroline went to bed extra early so she could get plenty of rest. She wanted to be the first one up so she could listen to her new stereo from Santa Claus. Jerry and Donna were up very late making all of the preparations, the last of which was putting a recording of "Jingle Bell Rock" on the stereo, ready for Caroline to discover.

Jerry and Donna tiptoed past Jake's room and then Caroline's on their way to their own for a little bit of sleep before the biggest and longest morning of the year. They just smiled at each other as the lights went out. As Jerry lay in bed beside his amazing wife, he began to count his blessings and thanked God for his wonderful family.

The young man thought about how he and Donna had been best friends growing up and how much he loved and depended on her. He could hardly recall a time in his life that they weren't together. Their families were members of the same church, and they had started dating while in high school. They married right out of college, just as Jerry started working for a prestigious accounting firm. Despite her college degree, Donna wanted to be a stay-at-home mom. She believed she was born to be a mother, and they both knew it.

Jerry recalled his excitement when he got the news that he was going to be a father. It was the best day of his life. When Caroline came along two years after his son, he could not have been prouder. His sweet little angel, Caroline, was the answer to so many prayers.

Just as Jerry began to drift off to sleep, he was blasted out of bed by the booming lyrics of "Jingle Bell Rock," coming from the family room. Caroline was up and ready for her big day with her new stereo… it was barely 4:00 a.m.!

Jerry could only smile as he lumbered down the hall toward the living room, his sweet Caroline, and a hot cup of coffee. Donna trailed just behind her husband as she sleepily sang along with the music.

Christmas Day faded into the New Year, and Jake and Caroline went back to school. Caroline just couldn't get enough of her new stereo. She regularly had friends over to listen to music, she was learning new songs, and she sang continuously, but Jerry and Donna began to notice a change in Caroline's behavior. She was just not the same sweet little girl.

It was most noticeable in the mornings, as Caroline woke up more often in a bad mood. Getting her ready for school had become all but impossible. As time went on, her behavior grew even worse. She constantly fought with her brother and was even getting in trouble at school. Then one day, Jerry received a call at his office. Donna was almost hysterical. Caroline had bitten a classmate and even cursed at her teacher. Caroline was not allowed to return to school until Jerry and Donna met with the school principal.

"How could this happen," Jerry snapped at Donna.

"I don't know," she snapped back.

Both blamed the other, and neither had a clue what was happening. They talked with Caroline but to no avail. It was as if she was a different human being, and they could only wonder how their sweet Caroline could have changed so radically in such a short period of time.

The following morning, Jerry and Donna met with Caroline's teacher and the school principal. Caroline's teacher was quite dismayed that in a few short months Caroline had gone from being very helpful, sweet, and caring to distant, selfish, and aggressive. No one had any answers, but they all agreed that counseling was a good first step.

Jerry and Donna called their pastor, who recommended a local child psychologist. They scheduled a session for the following day after school.

Jerry and Donna met with the psychologist alone first, and then Caroline spent about thirty minutes with the doctor. After the session, the doctor advised Jerry and Donna to think very hard about what had changed in Caroline's life. What was going on now that was not just a few months before? They searched their minds, but they came up with nothing.

A few weeks went by, and Caroline's behavior only worsened. She was still causing trouble at school, she was losing friends, and she didn't even seem to care, and the counseling sessions continued.

One morning, Jerry went into Caroline's room before she woke; he just sat there watching his little girl sleep. "She is so beautiful," he thought. "How could such a sweet and innocent child change into such a little terror?" he wondered. "How could this have happened?"

As he sat there in the semi-lit room in the still of the morning, he noticed a faint sound. As he looked around the room, he realized the sound was coming from Caroline's stereo. Jerry walked over to the stereo and listened closely to the music, but he couldn't quite make out the song. It sounded disturbingly aggressive and coarse. Turning the volume up, he almost leaped out of his skin.

"What is this?" he shouted as the music blasted. Jerry stood astonished as he listened to some of the vilest language he had ever heard, and it was all coming out of Caroline's stereo.

As it turned out, Donna had carefully chosen an "easy listening" radio station for Caroline to listen to at night. Little did she know that after midnight, the music genre changed to something much different. The lyrics to the songs that Caroline was hearing as she slept were filled with profanity and advocated everything from gross violence to murder and rape. It is little wonder that these verbal messages, repeated over and over, had inflicted such ill effects on such an innocent mind. After switching to a more appropriate choice of music, it wasn't long before Caroline returned to her normal self.

This story begs some questions:

- What music are you listening to?
- What kinds of books are you reading?
- What are you viewing on social media?
- What are you watching on television?
- What movies do you go see?
- What are you doing on the internet?
- What do you talk about with your friends or co-workers?
- And just as importantly, what are you saying to yourself?

This may seem overly simplistic, but it could not be more important. You've likely heard the saying, "you are what you eat." Well, it is infinitely more important for you to understand that you are absolutely what you *think*. You are indeed the sum total of your own thoughts, for better or for worse.

Your mind is the ultimate battleground of failure versus success, as well as good versus evil. Get used to it, and take it very seriously because what goes into your mind, if repeated often enough and with enough emotion, is ultimately expressed in outward physical action. Your journey to achieving the goals you have established for your life literally begins and ends with your ability to control what goes into your own two ears, as well as what you say to yourself. The importance of this cannot be overstated.

"Garbage in, garbage out" is a term that computer programmers use to emphasize the truth that you can't expect to get out any better than you put in, and it is the exact same phenomenon with the human mind. If you listen to foul language, gossip, or participate in defeatist or negative talk, your mind is literally infected with the ill-used words and thoughts.

Einstein once said, "A problem cannot be solved at the same level of understanding at which it was created." Well, I was raised in Georgia, and we say it a little differently there. "If you keep on doing what you've always done, you'll keep on gettin' what you always got."

Okay, so what does this all mean? If you don't like where you are in your life, then the first step to meaningful change begins with changing the way you think. You must guard what goes into your mind because it influences how you think and then, ultimately, how you act. Thoughts repeated often enough lead to action. Repeated action leads to the formation of habits, and our habits are the bedrock foundation of who we are, for better or worse.

The starting point for me was the Bible. I found that I really needed to hear from God. I recall listening to a local Christian radio station in Charlotte, and one of the hosts referred to the Bible as being the "owner's manual." With that in mind, I thought it might be a good idea to see what our "manufacturer" had to say about how He intended us to "run."

I began by looking up and writing down every verse I could find on building confidence, integrity, honesty, strength, wisdom, victory, persistence, overcoming doubt, and eliminating fear. I put these verses on three-by-five cards and displayed them where I could see them all day long. I did my best to commit them to memory. My favorite is Luke 18:1 (NIV), which tells us to "Always pray and not give up."

Something that has always been important to me is being very selective with the television news, including the talk shows and the news media I listen to. Most of it is just too negative. To this day, I diligently work to eliminate anything from my life that isn't positive and uplifting, and I can't emphasize enough how important this selection process is for me… and could be for you, as well.

At the beginning of this process, I went to the public library and read or checked out any motivational books I could find. Later on, I began building my own library. I tried very hard to get anything I could on audio so I could listen to it over and over as I drove in my car. Today, I still add to my collection and often buy both the paperback book and audio version of each title so I can get the full benefit of the information. My library includes books and audios by influencers, such as Les Brown, Og Mandino, Norman Vincent Peale, Darren Hardy, Jim Rohn, Dave Ramsey, Anthony Robbins, Brian Tracy, Earl Nightingale, Steven Covey, John Maxwell, the master Zig Ziglar, and others. When I can, I go to seminars and other live events so that I can hear these leaders speak in person, shake their hands, and let them know how they have positively affected my life.

It's simple. Control what goes into your mind, and you will take better control of your life and your destiny.

The Big Idea

- Your mind is the battleground of success versus failure.
- If you want to improve your life, you must change the way that you think.
- Continually feed your mind positive information.

Chapter 10
We Become What We Think About

"We become what we think about most of the time,
and that's the strangest secret."
—Earl Nightingale

MANY years ago, I came across "The Strangest Secret," by Earl Nightingale. In this recording, Nightingale shared six simple words that can change and transform the lives of anyone and everyone who truly understands them and consciously implements them. He described these words as being "the key to success and the key to failure." You may ask how anything can be both the key to success *and* the key to failure. This is true because it depends on how you choose to use them.

It is an undeniable fact that you can use these words as the foundation to improve any and every part of your life. If you fully understand these words and positively implement them, they can help you achieve any desire or dream you may have. Or, if ignored, they can and will lead you to a life of struggle, misery, and possibly even destruction. What exactly are these six words? They are simply, *"we become what we think about."*

Now, you might ask yourself, "so, does this mean that if we think about elephants or baboons that we will somehow *become* an elephant or a baboon?" Well, obviously not. But as it relates to the workings of the human mind, understanding that "we become what we think about," is the key that unlocks the mysteries of behavioral success and failure in our lives here on earth.

Consider this... the human mind is responsible for conceiving and creating every single manmade *thing*, as well as every manmade *condition* on this planet. Everything you see and use in your day-to-day life, which was made by the hand of man, had its beginnings as an idea and is therefore a product of the human mind. From controlling fire and the invention of the wheel to the beds we sleep in, the cars we drive, the computers we use, the cell phones we carry, and the medical procedures that cure disease and save lives, everything that improves our lives here on earth had their beginnings as seeds planted in the human mind.

Conversely, the human mind is equally responsible for every negative man-made thing and condition that is in our existence. And so, the choice is ours. We can use what God gave us to accomplish every positive task we can conceive, or we can use this same exact gift in a negative fashion, bringing about pain, suffering, misery, and ultimately, our own destruction.

Neuroscientists describe the human brain as the most complicated device ever discovered in the universe. And to this day, there are no plausible theories of how the brain works. Inside your brain, over 100,000 chemical reactions take place every single second. There are more connections in one cubic millimeter of brain tissue than there are stars in the Milky Way galaxy. In early pregnancy, the brain of a human fetus develops neurons at the rate of 250,000 per minute. Over the course of an average lifetime, our brains retain up to 1,000,000,000,000,000 (one quadrillion) pieces of information, and every single day, we have about 70,000 different thoughts. Some of these thoughts are positive in nature, and some are negative. Every time you learn or experience something new, the structure of your brain alters and changes, and with every new memory you have, new brain connections are formed. Our brains are constantly adapting to the thoughts we have and to the ever evolving and changing conditions of our lives. It is for this reason we *must* have control over what goes into our minds and, ultimately, how we think.

The plain and simple fact is that the *dominant* thoughts of our minds lead us to take action. Thus, we continually move in the direction of what we think about most. So, as a consequence, we do or carry out, what we think about most. As Nightingale explains, "Throughout history, the great wise men, teachers, philosophers, and prophets have disagreed with one another on many different things. It is only on this one point that they are in complete and unanimous agreement. The key to success and the key to failure is *we become what we think about*... It was first promulgated by some of the earliest wise men, and it appears again and again throughout the Bible. But very few have learned it or understand it. That is why it is so strange and for some equally strange reason remains a secret... This information is enormously valuable to us if we really understand it and apply it."

There is indeed a long and impressive list of those throughout the history of humankind who have discovered and shared that we do, in fact, become what we think about. Possibly beginning with "The Maxims of Ptahhotep," an advisor of the Egyptian Pharaoh Isesi who left words of wisdom for us to discover in approximately 2400 B.C. His writings left no doubt that an excellent life involves controlling the way we think.

In addition to the Ancient Egyptians, the philosopher Plato, in about 400 B.C., said, "For a man to conquer himself is the first and noblest of all victories." The Bible is filled with example after example of the fact that we are instructed to feed our minds with the pure, the powerful, and the positive and advises us to control the way we think. Roman Emperor Marcus Aurelius wrote in his life's work, *The Meditations of Marcus Aurelius*, around 160 A.D., "A man's life is what his thoughts make it" and "It is all within yourself, in your way of thinking."

My earliest understanding of this truth was through reading Zig Ziglar's, *See You At The Top*, Earl Nightingale's, *The Strangest Secret*, and Dr. Norman Vincent Peale's, *The Power of Positive Thinking*. It is through studying the works of these three great men that I have come to confirm the power of what they teach, which is that clarity of mind, purpose, and even one's whole self can be achieved by anyone who chooses to follow and discern this great and simple mantra: *We become what we think about.*

In modern times, we have irrefutable confirmation that we indeed *become what we think about* through such great minds as psychologist William James who said, "The greatest discovery of my generation is that human beings can alter their lives by altering their attitudes of mind… If you only care enough for a result, you will almost certainly obtain it. If you wish to be rich, you will be rich. If you wish to be learned, you will be learned. If you wish to be good, you will be good… Only you must then really wish these things and wish them exclusively and not wish at the same time a hundred other things just as strongly."

It is an unquestionable and undeniable fact that we indeed become what we think about. If we feed our minds with positive thoughts, our lives will move in a positive direction. If we choose to dwell on the negative aspects of life, our lives will move in a negative direction. And in the absence of a specific goal in life, our mind will take on the randomness that exists all around us. As a result, our lives will be filled with uncertainty, misunderstanding, anxiety, worry, and fear. The lack of a clear and definite plan can only lead to a life of wandering aimlessly, much like a ship without a course or destination in mind.

Know in your heart that you have a mind with abilities far beyond your comprehension. You have the ability to achieve any goal you purposefully set your mind upon. Begin today and right where you are. Expand your vision of what is possible for your life, and trust that you have the talent and ability to achieve any goal or dream you may have for your life.

Never fall into the trap of believing the lie that you do not have what it takes to achieve what it is that you dream of. Know in your heart that you were created for a *specific purpose*, but it is up to you to do the work to uncover it, nurture it, and fulfill it. No one can fulfill your purpose but you, and what it is that you are meant to accomplish will not get done unless you do it.

Ask yourself this question: Based on your current thoughts, what are you on the path to become, and in what direction will that lead your life?

Whether you accept it or not or even like it or not, we do indeed *become what we think about*, so with specific intention, place your mind and your thoughts on what it is that you want to accomplish and the kind of life you want to live.

Choose to step out of the ordinary and live a life of abundance, prosperity, and joy. Expand your vision of what is possible for your life, and strive every day to live up to your full potential. Choose a life of balance and freedom and helping others. Choose to be a friend and mentor at every opportunity. Make a conscious effort to be an outstanding and loving parent and spouse. Learn to focus on being and doing your best. Choose to live without the limitations that we too often place on ourselves. Choose to live a life of meaning and purpose. Make a conscious decision to seek out and do whatever is good and right and to live with honesty, character, and integrity.

Know that you have the power within you to *specifically choose* in advance the direction of your life... or, you can choose nothing and be tossed around by culture and circumstance. The choice is yours...

The Big Idea

- Continually feed your mind positive thoughts.
- Focus on building character, honesty, and integrity.
- Know that you have abilities far beyond your comprehension.

Chapter 11
Look at Yourself First

"If you could kick the person in the pants responsible for most of your troubles, you wouldn't sit for a month."
—Theodore Rosevelt

I WILL not soon forget going to have lunch with a friend of mine from work one afternoon. He drove, and I sat in the front passenger seat. About a mile down the road, we noticed smoke coming from under the dash. Being quite alarmed by this we immediately pulled over to inspect the problem.

We anxiously exited the car with visions of it bursting into flames at any second. As my friend opened the hood, we held our breaths, expecting to see a massive plume of smoke come billowing out of the engine compartment, but there was no smoke. We looked back inside the vehicle and under the dash, but, again, there was no smoke. We started the engine and reinspected everything; still, no smoke.

Confused but relieved, we got back on the road and headed for the restaurant. As we drove, we again noticed smoke building up under the dash. This time, we pulled into a parking lot and left the engine running as we both inspected every inch of the car. We looked under the hood, under the car, under the dash, and everywhere else inside the car. Nothing. We even looked in the trunk, but again, there was no smoke.

Baffled, we had no recourse but to get back in the car. We just sat there puzzled with the engine running, the doors closed, and the windows up. We waited in silence for a couple of minutes, and sure enough, we again noticed the smoke rising from underneath the dash. All of a sudden, my friend screamed something and bolted out of the car. When I made my way around to the driver's side, my friend was hopping and jumping around the parking lot, frantically yelling something. All I could do was laugh at him because he looked like a nut.

Then, I realized what he was yelling. "My pants are on *fire!*" It was then I noticed the bottom of one of his pant legs had burned away. Recalling my Boy Scout training, I immediately sprang into action and drenched my friend's pant leg with my half-empty bottle of Coke... only glad to help!

As he cleaned himself up, my rattled friend asked, "Did you have to drench me with Coke?" I assured him that the Coke was better than Plan B, and we finally made our way to the restaurant.

It turned out that just before we had left, my friend had lit a cigarette for a co-worker and tossed the match down, not realizing that it had landed in the cuff of his pants. The smoldering ember from the match gradually burned away the cotton and wool fabric, causing the smoke and then eventually, the fire.

Albert Einstein once said, "A man must cease attributing his problems to his environment, and learn again to exercise his will, his personal responsibility." Let's face it, we all have problems in our lives that need to be solved, and it is amazing the lengths we go to, looking elsewhere and blaming anyone and everyone except ourselves for the problems we create or allow into our lives. Why is it that when problems arise, we tend to instinctively look at anything and everything but ourselves for the cause?

Life's challenges have a way of introducing us to the best and worst parts of ourselves. When things go well, we want to take the credit, but when things go wrong, we tend to point fingers and blame. It's like putting the wrong address into your GPS and then blaming the GPS for getting you lost!

It is important to understand that when we blame others for the problems we have in our lives, we are actually yielding control of our lives to others. When problems arise, don't look for whom you can blame; instead, take ownership of it and begin to find the solution. These *self-inflicted* wounds can be tough to handle, and it's never easy to admit fault. Nonetheless, when we make mistakes, we need to admit them, learn from them, and move on.

It is important to be diligent and slightly self-critical in an effort to become aware of our own shortcomings and being honest with yourself about them is key. Always be mindful of the areas in your life where you need to grow and improve. The only way we can progress in our lives is to take ownership of ourselves and realize we are all responsible for the successes or failures in our own lives.

Don't get me wrong. Sometimes our problems are the fault of others. There is no question about that, but we should make it a point to first look at ourselves and our own thoughts, actions, and behaviors, rather than immediately blaming others for the problems we face.

There is no getting around the fact that we all make errors in judgment, but it is crucial to always look for ways to learn from our mistakes. When we are faced with an issue, we should ask ourselves what we could do differently (or better) to have the best possible outcome. Beyond this we should also seek to understand what we could have done to prevent the problem entirely... After all, problems are nearly always much easier to prevent than to solve.

If your relationships are a mess, if you give up too soon, if you have problems telling the truth, if you continually have character issues, if you feel inferior to others, if you are always broke, or if you are not living up to what you know you are capable of, then ask the most important question you can ever ask of yourself. *Why?*

Take an intentionally close look at yourself and the condition of your life. As Einstein explained, this is about exercising personal responsibility and taking ownership of yourself and understanding that *you* are in control of your own life.

I love the point Zig Ziglar makes when he asks, "Is there anything that you can do *right now*, at this moment, to make your life *worse?*" I don't know about you, but I can think of about a hundred things I could do right now to make my life worse. Zig then points out, "If there is something that you can do right now, at this moment, to make your life worse, then there is obviously something that you can do right now to make your life *better.*"

The obvious point is that you are absolutely in control of your own life and, thus, in control of your own future, so take hold of the reins of your life and be in control. Any part of your life that you know needs to be improved upon, ask yourself *why* it needs improvement and then ask *what* you can *do* to improve it. Then follow through, *take action*, and go do it with the mindset of *no excuses and no regrets.*

Never allow yourself to settle for less than you know you can be. Never allow yourself to fall into the trap of believing, "Oh well, that's just how I am" or "I'm only human" when you know that you are better than your current position or circumstances. An excellent life is about taking an intimate look at your life as it exists right now, and with *critical honesty*, doing what it takes to improve.

I encourage you to lay down for yourself a new foundation, a rock-solid foundation of increased character, honesty, and wisdom. Be proud of who you are, and work every day to take ownership and responsibility for the choices and decisions you make.

Never settle for less than you know you can be. Never allow faults of your character to get the best of you. Always search for wisdom from others and seek out quality mentors. Continually search for ways to improve and move yourself forward, ever closer to becoming the person you know you are fully capable of being. Strive to take on positive virtues and live out positive values. Be intentional and deliberate about how you approach every area of your life, and work to be fully self-aware. Learn to exercise your will, be in control, and take complete responsibility for every aspect of your life. Do this, and you will most certainly live a more joyful, more fulfilling, prosperous, and *excellent life.*

The Big Idea

• When problems arise, look at yourself first.
• Avoid playing the blame game.
• Improve your character so faults don't get the best of you.

Chapter 12
Overcoming Our Circumstances

"Adversity introduces a man to himself"
—Albert Einstein

THAT unmistakable voice. Close your eyes and listen inside your mind to the harmonious and soothing voice attached to the words, "This is *CNN*" or the infamous line from *Star Wars* where Darth Vader says to Luke Skywalker, "No, *I* am your father."

Is there anyone on earth with a richer, more distinctive, or more authoritative voice? I believe we could argue that James Earl Jones has one of the most iconic and recognizable voices of all time, but it wasn't always this way…

"Mm… mm… my n—n—name i—is J—J—J—James," he stuttered. That is what people heard when a young James Earl Jones attempted to speak. Most people do not realize that from the time he started elementary school until he was in high school, James Earl Jones lived with functional mutism. For eight years, James remained silent and chose not to speak to avoid the pain and embarrassment of his uncontrollable stuttering.

It was while in high school that James finally gained the motivation and confidence necessary to stand up to this overwhelming and debilitating condition. With patience and resolve, young James practiced reading poetry in front of his class. Over and over, he would attempt to read; over and over, he would get stuck on the words; over and over, he dealt with the embarrassment; over and over, he felt the shame; and over and over, he failed, but, gaining a measure of confidence with each passing day, and with every repetition. Day after day, week after week, for months on end, he read, practiced, and focused on his speech until he was able to work through his challenge, ultimately finding his voice... and what a voice it turned out to be!

Indeed, his willingness to fail and his resolve to stand up to and overcome his challenge is what slowly built his confidence and gave him the courage and strength necessary to rise above his fears, placing him firmly in control of his future. The choice he made to work through his fears, beyond any doubt, irrevocably altered and changed his view of what was possible for his life. Indeed, none of his successes would have been achieved without a burning desire to overcome the most challenging obstacle of his young life.

You have to ask yourself, what kind of future was in store for a poor, African-American kid from small-town Mississippi, growing up in the 1930s and '40s, who wouldn't speak, and when he did speak, the words barely came out. If not for the encouragement and kind mentoring of a great teacher and the courage and resolve of James himself, his future would have been bleak. It was only because of his willingness to stand up to his inner demons that he gradually worked up the courage necessary to speak, no matter what came out and no matter how long it took.

Though only those closest to him may realize it, he still, on occasion, stutters. During his long and esteemed career, James Earl Jones has won three Emmy Awards, two Tony Awards, a Grammy Award, and even an Academy Award. He and his magnificent voice will live on forever through his work in movies, theatre, and television.

> *"One who gains strength by overcoming obstacles possesses*
> *the only strength which can overcome adversity."*
> *–Albert Schweitzer*

Circumstances, obstacles, barriers, challenges, limitations, adversities, trials, or disadvantages... no matter what you call them, we all face them. They are simply part of life.

No two people ever walk the same path or have the same challenges or circumstances. Know that whatever negative situation in which you find yourself, with the correct perspective, patience, and discipline, it can be dealt with and ultimately overcome. A fundamental aspect of living an excellent life is discerning the subtle yet powerful lessons from life's challenges and failures. We must understand that true and lasting success is ultimately achieved, not by the absence of challenges or failures, but rather in our ability to face them, work through them, and ultimately overcome them.

Whether it is poverty, illiteracy, a physical limitation, or nearly any other challenge or negative circumstance, you have within you the ability, determination, and strength of will to, with time and patience, work through it. Know that failure itself is nothing more than a temporary obstacle to be conquered.

Franklin Roosevelt had polio; multi-billionaire entrepreneur Richard Branson has dyslexia; Winston Churchill was a political outcast; Thomas Edison had almost no formal education; Stephen Hawking had ALS; Bill Gates's first business failed; Tyler Perry twice attempted suicide; Charles Dickens had epilepsy; Jim Carrey grew up poor and was sometimes homeless; Oprah Winfrey lost a child at fourteen; Walt Disney suffered from depression; Stephen Spielberg was twice rejected from film school, and Beethoven was deaf. All of these people were or are ultra-successful in their fields. They all suffered through difficult and sometimes tragic circumstances but did not allow those circumstances to become the defining characteristic of their lives. They all overcame their challenges and hardships and, in the process of doing so, have become inspirations to those who similarly struggle or suffer.

Like them, we should never allow ourselves to view the negative circumstances in our lives as barriers that would prevent us from achieving; rather, our challenges and trials should be viewed as weights to be lifted to make us stronger and move us forward.

You see, our challenge is not merely to overcome the individual circumstances within our lives, but rather to overcome *ourselves*. We think negatively and wonder why we feel anger and resentment. We focus on how we feel we have been wronged and become a victim in search of an oppressor. We focus on our failures instead of the lessons to be learned. We compare ourselves to others, not understanding that everyone's path is different. We look around us and focus on what we believe we lack instead of seeing what we have been given. We labor to improve the individual circumstances we face and put out the "fires" in our lives instead of looking deep within ourselves and seeking to build our character, wisdom, integrity, our resolve, strength of will, and our faith.

Understand that when we accept our negative circumstances as being too trying, too difficult, or just a part of who we are, we then convince ourselves that they cannot to be overcome. When we do this, when we accept the negative circumstances in our lives as being unmanageable, unsurpassable, or unchangeable, we then become a prisoner to them. By our own choosing, we turn what has the potential to make us stronger and lead us to a life of excellence and abundance into something that stifles our growth, binds us, and limits our future, sometimes irrevocably. When we allow this to happen, we literally trap ourselves within our circumstances, seeing no escape, when, in actuality, all it takes to overcome them is to believe the obstacle itself exists to be conquered.

Ask yourself *why* you are faced with the negative circumstance in which you find yourself. Objectively ask yourself what you could have done differently and continually seek to understand what caused you to be where you are in your life. Do this, not to search for whom to blame, but rather to discover the valuable lessons to be learned which are embedded within the circumstance.

It may surprise you to know there is a very basic but necessary process that each and every one of us must go through to overcome the obstacles that challenge us in our everyday lives. It is, quite simply, *fail, learn,* and *repeat.*

Winston Churchill said, "Success is stumbling from failure to failure with no loss of enthusiasm." You see, no one ever starts out in life as successful and living a life of abundance and excellence. It is only through consistent and persistent effort that it is possible to cast aside what holds us back. For the vast majority, it's only through a continuous willingness to fail and meticulously learning from our mistakes and failures that a high level of successful achievement is attainable or even possible. An interesting fact is that the earlier in life we learn to work to overcome the challenges we face, the easier it tends to be to understand the lessons within the challenge and learn from them. By contrast, if we find ourselves dealing with the same issues repeatedly throughout our lives or we seem to find ourselves moving from one set of challenges to the next because we have never truly learned the lessons they teach, the more difficult they can be to overcome. But make no mistake, at any age and at any phase of life, the challenges and obstacles you face can indeed be overcome. Never allow yourself to believe otherwise.

> *"Anyone can do just about anything with himself that he really wants to and makes up his mind to do. We are capable of greater things than we realize."*
> *–Norman Vincent Peale*

Know that if you were to pull back the veil of almost any successful, excellent life, you would undoubtedly find that the foundation of excellence was achieved through very basic, sometimes extremely difficult, and even tragic challenges and failures. Most people view a successful or excellent life as being a life without deep struggles or failure, or they view success as being the absence of failure. I would argue those individuals completely misunderstand how true success is actually achieved.

The fruits of our successes in life are most typically born out of our obstacles, struggles, challenges, setbacks, and yes, even our most difficult and crushing trials and failures. In fact, failure and learning from our mistakes might be *the* necessary and unavoidable ingredient for long-term achievement and success. The very foundation of the most extraordinarily successful people throughout history is routinely built atop the wreckage of the many hard-learned lessons and challenges from their pasts.

Understand that the manner in which we approach and deal with the challenging circumstances of life, how we handle failure, and how we learn from our own mistakes, setbacks, and failures is as essential to our development and inward growth as oxygen is to life. It is impossible to have life without oxygen, and it is impossible to live a life of success and excellence without the internal strength and fortitude we gain from experiencing the most challenging circumstances of life. Indeed, without the lessons learned from our failures in life, true and lasting success is seldom attainable or even possible.

You see, to achieve the virtue of possessing good judgment, it is necessary to have first learned the invaluable and hard-earned lesson of possessing bad judgment. To live with humility, we must struggle and learn to overcome pride and self-centeredness. To achieve discipline in our lives, we must first overcome apathy and complacency. And to be a person who values justice, we have got to work to overcome and stifle the injustices in our own lives.

Don't misunderstand. I am in no way suggesting that we should seek out challenges to overcome, trials to endure, or obstacles to needlessly face. There will always be an abundance of difficult circumstances in life to be dealt with. As soon as you think to yourself "I have life in the palm of my hand," that is the moment you could be introduced to the greatest challenge of your life.

What I *am* saying is to always be prepared—in your heart and mind—for what lies around the next corner and to be relentlessly mindful of the areas of your character that leave you vulnerable. Learn to be more self-aware, slightly self-critical, and focused on the larger picture of life's challenges. *Learn how to learn* from the negative circumstances you face, thus becoming more aware of *why* you faced a particular challenge in the first place. Learning from our mistakes is how we become better armed to face similar challenges in the future. Understand that *facing* and diligently *working to overcome* the many challenges of life is what builds our character, increases our confidence, strengthens our resolve, and creates true and lasting hope for the future.

What Isaac Newton said is true: "For every action, there is an equal and opposite reaction." Thus, darkness can only be driven out by light, evil is overcome by good, and the opposite of hate is love. Eliminating hate from your life can only be accomplished by becoming more loving, and bad habits can only be subdued by diligently working to build good habits. In the same manner, ignorance is replaced by knowledge, fear is replaced by courage, and weakness is cast aside by strength.

I challenge you to closely examine the lives of those who have **excelled**, who have achieved excellence, and who you look up to and admire. Learn about not just their successes but also their challenges, setbacks, and failures. Learn about the difficulties they had to overcome to become great. Learn about the instances in their lives when they struggled and dealt with trials, difficulties, and hard times. Learn about *how* they dealt with the challenges they faced, the self-doubt they endured, and the lessons they ultimately learned, which allowed them to break through to a life of achievement, reward, substance, abundance, and improved moral character.

Know that the common denominator for nearly every successful, excellent life is not the easy and effortless road from one success to another, as some may think. Rather, for most of us, success and excellence in life lies buried deep within our obstacles, challenges, self-doubts, and fears and how we process them, study them, learn from them, and with faithful diligence, ultimately overcome and master them. For many, including James Earl Jones, their ultimate success is often born out of the very obstacle and challenge they faced. Indeed, it is not at all unusual that our life's greatest struggle becomes refined and distilled into the seed of life's greatest accomplishment.

Show me someone who has intimately learned the secrets of understanding and dealing with the ongoing circumstances of life, including standing up to and facing their deepest insecurities, fears, and failures, and I will show you someone who will grow to achieve any task they set their mind to. Show me someone who has learned the secrets of overcoming *themselves*, and thus, with patience and discipline, built the internal strength and fortitude necessary to work through the many challenges they face, and I will show you someone who will one day be an inspiration and mentor to the masses and, in due course, the master of their own destiny.

The Big Idea

- Learning from failure is a necessary ingredient for success.
- Life's obstacles exist to be overcome.
- Your greatest struggles can lead to your greatest accomplishments.

Chapter 13
Knowing True Freedom

"Education is the key to unlock the golden door of freedom."
—George Washington Carver

SONYA cried uncontrollably as she sat alone in her cold, dimly lit bedroom. "How could he do this to us?" she begged. "How will I ever make it through this?" she wondered aloud. Her heart was completely broken as she thought about her two young boys, asleep down the hall. "How can I tell them what he has done? They will never understand. They love their father so much! How could he do this to us? Doesn't he love us? Doesn't he care about us?" she cried out.

"What's wrong, Mama?" Curtis, her oldest son, called out from down the hall.

"Get back in bed," she warned, trying to sound strong and in control. Her voice was breaking as she desperately tried to hold back the tears. "You better get back to bed, boy!" she exclaimed.

"Yes, Mama," he answered.

Her eyes were swollen nearly shut from the tears—from crying so hard she could hardly breathe. "I can't make it through this," she mumbled. Hardly able to see, she wiped her face with her sleeve. Her knees buckled as she attempted to stand; she felt so alone, so scared and defeated. An overwhelming wave of depression consumed her. "I just want to lie down and die," she thought to herself. Still crying, she buried her face in the pillow as she lay across the empty, old wood-framed bed. Exhausted and emotionally spent, she drifted off to sleep.

Hours later, daylight filled the room, spilling in through the half-covered window. The bright sun enveloped her like a warm blanket. "I know that's you, God," she said to herself. "Just leave me be," she said aloud. She lay on her back with the glowing sunlight across her face, trying not to think about the uncertain future she was forced to accept.

As she struggled to gather herself, she could hear her two boys, Curtis, ten, and Benny, who had just turned eight, arguing in the kitchen. "Them boys are always at each other," she thought. "How am I gonna face those boys?" she wondered. "Y'all hush now!" she warned.

Dragging herself from the bed, she was happy to hear the boys, even if they were arguing. It was a welcome distraction from the pain. "At least I know where I stand with them," she thought. She made her way down the hall, hardly noticing the cold wooden floor on her bare feet. Adjusting her tattered blue robe, she folded her arms across her chest, took a deep breath, and greeted the boys. "Good morning, boys," she announced.

"Who were you talkin' to last night, Mama?" Benny asked.

"I wasn't talkin' to no one," she replied.

"It sho was loud for nobody to be talkin'," Curtis jumped in.

"Just get yo breakfast," she snapped back as she kissed Benny on the top of the head, pretending it was just another day.

She unconsciously hugged them harder and longer than usual as they started out for school. "What's wrong, Mama?" Curtis asked knowingly.

"Nothin'," she replied. "Everything's fine."

"Did Daddy come home last night?" Benny asked.

"Y'all just get on to school," she urged. Curtis noticed the tears welling up in her eyes as she hugged them once again. He said nothing else to her as he tugged at his younger brother's arm.

"Come on, Benny. We don't wanna be late again." While Benny ran ahead, Curtis looked back toward his mother as she sat on the bottom step of the porch with her face in her hands.

Sonya sat transfixed and sobbing as she thought back over her life, wondering how things could have gone so wrong. "How did I end up here?" she thought, her mind racing as she reflected back over her life.

Married at only thirteen to a man much older than she—more than twice her age. She had thought that being married would give her freedom... a childish, romantic dream gone wrong—so horribly wrong. "I should have known," she mumbled to herself. "What does a grown man want with a little girl anyway?" she sobbed. "What's wrong with him?... What's wrong with me?" she cried out.

As Sonya picked herself up and walked back into the empty, cold house, she cried out, "God, help me! Please help me! Why is this happening to me?"

She recalled a poem, "Yourself to Blame," which she thought about from time to time. As tears ran down her face, she began to recite the words of Mayme White Miller.

> *If things go bad for you*
> *And make you a bit ashamed*
> *Often you will find out that*
> *You have yourself to blame*
>
> ~
>
> *Swiftly we ran to mischief*
> *And then the bad luck came*
> *Why do we fault others?*
> *We have ourselves to blame*
>
> ~

Whatever happens to us,
Here is what we say
"Had it not been for so-and-so
Things wouldn't have gone that way."

~

And if you are short of friends,
I'll tell you what to do
Make an examination,
You'll find the faults in you...

~

You are the captain of your ship,
So agree with the same
If you travel downward
You have yourself to blame.

Sonya had always battled depression, and this new challenge seemed completely hopeless, but as she thought about the words in the poem, she realized she had a choice to make. She could simply blame her husband for her plight and become a *victim* all over again, or she could find a way to take control of her life and work to overcome the challenges she was facing.

It was a few days later when Sonya told Curtis and Benny their father would not be living with them anymore.

"Why not?" questioned Benny. It was the strange matter-of-fact manner of her words that alarmed him the most. "What did I do to make him not want to live with us?" he asked.

"Nothing, Benny," she assured.

"But I love him," he replied.

"And your father loves you too. Very much."

"Then why can't he live with us? I'll be good!" he cried out.

"Boys, listen to me, and you listen good," she said. "Neither of you have done anything wrong. Your father has done some very bad things, and he just can't live with us anymore. And he won't ever be coming back. But we are going to be fine; as long as we have each other and we trust in God, we will all be just fine."

Somehow, Curtis and Benny understood, and they believed their mother's words. They would be fine, but that didn't make them stop wondering where their father was or why he wouldn't be coming back home. Eventually, the boys learned that their father could not live with them because he had another family, which they had not known about. Despite the inevitable consequences and the uncertainty of what lay ahead, Sonya was strong enough to tell him that he had lost the right to be a part of their lives and that he had to go.

Being one of twenty-four children, Sonya had married young as a way to get out of a desperate home life. She had only a third-grade education, couldn't read, and had no professional skills. There seemed to be no reason to believe that she would be able to support herself, much less two young sons, but she knew in her heart they would make it because they *had* to make it. She would not accept anything less. She was strong, hardworking, knew how to save money, and most importantly, possessed an attitude that would not allow her to quit. But her biggest asset was her unwavering and complete faith in God.

As time went on, Sonya and the boys settled into their new life without their husband and father. Even though she had to work long, hard hours as a maid, cleaning two and even three homes per day to keep food on the table, clothes on their backs, and a roof over their heads, they were making it. Sonya did everything she could do to earn money, save that money, and make it through another day, but she was very concerned about the boys. Little Benny was the worst student in his class, failing most of his subjects, and Curtis wasn't doing much better. She knew that if this did not change, her two boys would face a hard and uncertain future.

The Turning Point

It was while working in the homes of wealthy families that Sonya began to notice that these people seemed to *think* differently than others she had been around. It was evident to her that they placed major importance on education and spent their time wisely. Their children studied and did their homework when they got home from school instead of going out to play or watching television. They read books and had discussions about global current events around the dinner table. She saw how they constructed their lives in a way that would all but guarantee a successful future—and thus freedom from the challenges of illiteracy and poverty.

> *"If someone is going down the wrong road,*
> *they don't need motivation to speed them up;*
> *they need education to turn them around."*
> —*Jim Rohn*

Sonya also noticed these individuals were not that different from her, and she reasoned that if they could live this type of life, then maybe she could, too. Sonya began to understand that success in life was not about chance, luck, or the randomness of birth. Rather, it was about making *intentional* choices and decisions, which would systematically move her life in a predictably positive direction. She now fully understood that her future—and the future of her two young boys—was indeed in her hands, and the first step toward a life of freedom and independence was to develop the positive habits necessary to make it possible.

Sonya cultivated these new positive habits and taught her boys a different way of thinking, acting, and viewing themselves. This experience radically altered and improved Sonya's and the boys' view of what they believed possible for their lives.

> *"Education is the movement from darkness to light."*
> —*Allen Bloom*

What do you think of when you hear the word *freedom?* Freedom is the right or ability to live life in any manner we may choose, within the law. In a free society, each one of us has the freedom to move our lives in any direction we choose. We can deliberately move our lives in a *positive* direction, or we can just as easily move our lives in a *negative* direction. Thus, freedom is a two-edged sword, which we can use to our advantage or, conversely, to our ultimate disadvantage.

It is interesting that in a society where certain freedoms are guaranteed by law, that so many find themselves in bondage, not merely by freedoms being taken from them, but by not fully understanding their freedoms and misusing them or, by abdication, giving them away.

You see, true freedom is not merely something that is granted by a government; rather, it is declared and claimed by each of us as individuals. Sure, a government can write into law that we have certain freedoms or rights, such as with religion, speech, voting, equal justice, owning property, and so on. But it is important to understand that *true* freedom and the ability to live an excellent life lies within the seemingly small choices and decisions we all make as individuals.

We all make choices in life. We can choose to live *disciplined* or *undisciplined* lives, and we can choose to build *positive* or *negative* habits. By choosing to be disciplined and living with positive habits, we move our lives forward in a predictably positive direction. By contrast, when we choose to be undisciplined and form negative habits, we are unconsciously choosing a life of dependence and even bondage.

Among the greatest gifts we can give to ourselves is one we claim the moment we choose to be *self-reliant.* By choosing to be self-reliant, thus making a *conscious choice* to cast aside dependence on others, we are, in fact choosing a path towards freedom. Absolute freedom can only be achieved by looking deep within ourselves to solve the issues and challenges each of us faces in our lives. No one can do this for us. It is a requirement of an excellent life to understand that we are all the "captains of our own ships," in control of our own futures.

Do not misunderstand me. Being self-reliant is in no way about pounding our chests and attempting to prove to ourselves (or others) that we do not need help, guidance, or direction. Nor does being self-reliant mean we are in any way excluding God from the important choices and decisions we make in our lives. Far from it. Being self-reliant in this context is about *choosing for ourselves* the path we will take in life, as well as making intentional choices about who and what we will serve.

In fact, I will argue that fully and completely trusting in God in a world continually trying to prove He is irrelevant or does not exist is one of life's greatest accomplishments. It is up to each and every one of us to be self-reliant, with God's continual and unconditional guidance and direction. As Psalm 37:5 (NLT) says, "Commit everything you do to the Lord. Trust Him, and he will help you."

One of Two Paths

As time went on, Sonya vowed to help her two young boys understand that life is about choices, choosing between one of two paths in life—one easy, the other much more difficult. But which was which?

Just think for a second about the uphill struggle Sonya faced. There she was with only a third-grade education, two young sons to support, no husband, no child support, no skills, no family to help her, and to top it all off, she couldn't even read. Living in the poverty-stricken inner-city of Detroit, what kind of future would you expect for Sonya and her children? There is no doubt the logical bet would have been a future of continual government assistance, illiteracy, poverty, and all of the associated negative effects that nearly always follow.

With the struggle Sonya faced, it would have been easy to just let the boys do as they pleased. After all, hadn't they already been through enough? With her working long, hard days, sometimes until late in the evening, all Sonya felt like doing when she got home was eating and going straight to bed, and who could blame her? The work she was doing was physically demanding, and she spent long hard hours on her feet. Who would expect anything more from her than to just get by, let the boys fend for themselves, and hope for some kind of a miracle? After all, there were plenty of kids in the neighborhood for them to play with, there were other adults to watch after them, if necessary… they'd be fine. Things usually work out somehow… don't they?

Sonya knew the key to her two young boys' futures was indeed a difficult road in the short term, but she knew this more difficult road would be the only way for them to be lifted out of dependence and poverty to a life of freedom and self-reliance. She knew beyond any doubt that the way out of their desperate situation was found *within themselves*, by making sure the boys developed positive habits and received the best education possible. And they needed to start immediately.

The first of many new habits was for the boys to do their homework as soon as they got home from school, limit television to just three programs per week, and ensure they read two books per week. Plus, they had to turn in a written report about each book to her… The boys had no idea their mother could not read, and for the time being, that would remain her secret.

"Why are you so mean to us?" Curtis demanded.

"Why can't we go outside and play with our friends?" Benny shouted.

"Only three television programs per week?" Curtis questioned.

"You want us to read two books a week? Are you kidding? Nobody can read two books *a week*," Benny argued.

"You boys don't need so much television," Sonya calmly explained. "And yes, you can read two books a week. You boys weren't born to be failures; you can do it. And besides, if you can read, you can learn just about anything," she added. "Boys, I want you to always remember, if you ask the Lord for something and you believe in your heart that He will do it, He will! You can do anything you set your mind to do."

Adjusting to the new schedule was tough, but the boys knew their mother was right, and besides, learning was fun, they reasoned.

The path Sonya chose for herself and for Curtis and Benny was indeed a difficult one—at the beginning, that is. This was a pivotal time for the small family, and it would have been easy for Sonya to have given in to the boys and let them have their way. It certainly would have been easier for her to simply let them occupy their time after school by watching television and playing with their friends, but what about their futures? What indeed would their futures be like if they didn't study and get the best educations possible?... And, what if they did?

The Rest of the Story...

Well, the story isn't finished yet. Sonya eventually learned to read and proved to be a great role model for her sons. She went on to get her GED and even went to college, receiving an honorary doctoral degree in 1994.

Curtis and young Benny did study hard and took their education very seriously. Both boys graduated from high school at the top of their classes. Curtis went on to get his engineering degree from the University of Michigan and to have a successful career with an aviation company. Little Benny made it to the Ivy League, received a full academic scholarship from Yale, and graduated in 1973. He went on to study medicine at the University of Michigan and, later, became the youngest director of Pediatric Neurosurgery at Johns Hopkins at the age of thirty-three.

After performing some of the most difficult and groundbreaking surgeries imaginable and saving countless lives, little Benny went on to author several bestselling books, which tell his amazing story. In 2016, Dr. Ben Carson ran for president of the United States and served as the seventeenth secretary of Housing and Urban Development.

Who could have ever imagined these two "throw away," inner-city kids from the hard streets of Detroit would grow up to *literally* become a rocket scientist and a brain surgeon? I will tell you who. Sonya Carson and the compassionate and loving God who gave them the confidence, talents, abilities, and gifts to do just that.

The story of Sonya Carson, as told in the book *Gifted Hands* by Dr. Ben Carson, should be required reading for every school-aged child, as well as every parent. The questions have to be asked… How many of us never live up to our full potential because we choose the *easy* path? How many of us live out our lives only scratching the surface of what we are capable of because we fail to put in the effort to uncover and fully develop the talents and abilities we are born with—the ones God gave us to use to fulfill a specific purpose?

Sonya Carson's story of courage and resolve is a shining example of what can be accomplished when we focus our thoughts on a goal, choose to be self-reliant, and are unwilling to give up or accept failure as an option.

> *"Trust in the Lord with all your heart and do not*
> *lean on your own understanding. In all your ways, acknowledge*
> *Him and He will make your path straight." Proverbs 3:5-6*

When we make the conscious decision to become self-reliant, trust God, believe in ourselves, and shut out or shun those who say it cannot be done, something nearly magical seems to happen

The courage that it took for Sonya Carson to take control of her life and the lives of her two sons was an act of faith, not merely faith in herself but faith in a loving and compassionate God.

Sonya believed with everything inside her that what the Bible says is true, that God is real, and that He loves each and every one of us. She also understood that God has given us all the talents, abilities, and gifts we need to carry out *His* plan for our lives.

It is tough to deny that what happened in their lives was indeed a miracle. And I would argue this same type of miracle is possible for anyone and everyone who, with faith, chooses to make it possible for themselves. Curtis and Ben (through their mother's insistence) intentionally and deliberately chose to work to develop the talents and abilities they *already possessed*, which were buried deep within them.

Dr. Ben Carson performed groundbreaking and amazing surgeries, which some argue no one else at that time was capable of performing. We *all* have abilities buried deep within us which are waiting to be realized and cultivated. All it takes is for us to take the first step in faith, to take the first steps in the direction of a fate we cannot see and do not yet fully conceive of or understand.

Let me ask you this: What does your future hold? What talents or abilities do you possess that have, up to this point, gone unnoticed, unnourished, or are yet to be developed? What miracle lies in your future, just waiting to be discovered? I encourage you to take the first step in faith toward the amazing achievements and accomplishments which are waiting for you to discover. You do not need to know the final destination, but with faith, take the first step, and be willing to allow God to lead your steps.

Side Note:

What the Carson family experienced is known as "upward mobility." Upward mobility is the ability for someone to move from one social or economic class to another. For millions of Americans who are born into poverty, upward mobility is proving to be an increasingly difficult, if not impossible, task to achieve. There have been endless studies and millions upon millions of dollars spent to determine exactly what changes need to be implemented to help individuals and families break the cycle of poverty and assist them in achieving the goal of economic freedom and self-reliance—or more plainly said, to be able to stand on their own two feet.

In 1964, President Lyndon Johnson declared a "war on poverty." Since then, our government has created some ninety-two different federal poverty programs. These programs cover such things as social services, housing, food aid, cash assistance, education, job training, and the list goes on. Since then, the United States has invested trillions of dollars in these programs. Some estimates place the total spent as being enough to nearly retire our national debt or up to three times more than America has spent fighting all of the wars in our nation's history *combined*, from the Revolutionary War through the War on Terror. And nearly six decades later, where do we stand?

The sad fact is there has been little to no measurable net result in lowering the rate of poverty or in raising the rate of upward mobility of those whom this money was intended to help. All that seems to have been accomplished is to reinforce in the minds of the poor that there is no hope for tomorrow, and their futures are going to be no different from their past. Ultimately, they see struggle and poverty as a way of life and, therefore, inevitable and unchangeable.

Those living in poverty lose hope because they do not see that they have a plausible path to overcome the many negative issues they face. So, as time moves forward and as children *of* poverty become adults *in* poverty, this endless cycle is repeated, generation after generation, and nothing meaningful ever changes or improves.

In the next chapter, we will take a close look at this seemingly unsolvable multi-generational issue and ponder what can be done about it.

The Big Idea

- Your future is in your hands.
- Develop positive habits.
- Make a conscious decision to be self-reliant.

Chapter 14
Upward Mobility

"If we are serious about providing upward mobility and building a skilled workforce, preschool is the place to begin."
—Madeline M. Kunin

THE last chapter discussed the amazing story of Ben Carson and how his mother, Sonya, lifted him and his brother out of a life of poverty and uncertainty and into a life of self-reliance and independence. There are many lessons to be learned from this story, but the most valuable lesson is that what she was able to accomplish can be duplicated. How she set about guiding herself and her two boys out of a life of poverty is a roadmap for anyone who finds themselves in a similar situation or for those working within government who have been tasked with solving such issues.

The American Dream

Make no mistake about it, solving the challenges of poverty and upward mobility is a complex undertaking, and there is no single solution to the problem. It has become increasingly evident that this issue has been made radically more complicated by the government itself through the creation of an intricate maze of programs whose missions seem to conflict with and even hinder one another. This is highlighted by a Spring 2019 study written by Michael Tanner, a senior fellow at the Cato Institute, who concludes, "The real problem isn't the poor, and it isn't society. It is the government."

For example, some government poverty programs offer support and much-needed aid while at the same time discouraging families from staying together and moving forward. It almost seems as though these programs have been created with the goal of ensuring that a certain percentage of the population remains in poverty and thus dependent on the government, rather than encouraging them to grow out of poverty to a life of self-reliance and independence.

Nearly everyone would agree there should be a safety net for those who cannot help themselves, and to me, this is an unarguable point. What is entirely arguable is precisely *how* to help those who find themselves in need of assistance. There is simply no reason for individuals and surely entire families to spend their entire lives in poverty, struggling to rise above it, trapped, generation after generation. So why is this happening, and what can be done about it?

Think for a minute about those whom you may have helped in your own life. I am sure you have noticed that *how* we go about helping others can often be as important as the assistance itself. And in some ways, it is more important. This is because the manner in which assistance is given can solve some problems while at the same time, create others.

If you examine how these federal and state programs offer assistance, there seems to be no real long-term plan to actually improve the lives of those receiving the assistance. For example, instead of providing a logical path out of poverty and toward upward mobility and self-reliance, the programs seem to merely make the poor more comfortable within their existing poverty, while gradually making them more dependent on the government.

Many programs offer help to single-parent families to the exclusion of intact families. Some programs even discourage families with two married parents. One startling result or unintended consequence is that the rate of children born outside of marriage has increased from 7 percent in 1964 when the War on Poverty began, to more than 40 percent today. Yes, this means over 40 percent of our nation's children are born to parents who are not married to each other, and we wonder why we have issues.

Sadly, we find ourselves in a much *worse* position to solve the issue of poverty and upward mobility today than before we spent over five decades and trillions of dollars attempting to solve it. Some would argue there has never been an actual, *honest* attempt to solve these important issues at all. This is because we, as a nation and through our federal government, seem to have approached the abolition of poverty with an eye toward creating more and more federal programs and growing government to the exclusion of achieving the goal at hand.

Am I saying that no one has actually been helped by all of this spending? Well, of course not, but it also depends on how you define *help*.

Have these programs given assistance to people who are in need? Yes.

Has the money spent through these programs helped the recipients to put roofs over their heads, food on their tables, or to go to school? Absolutely—no question about it.

Is spending money to help the poor the right thing to do?

There is no doubt about that either. But layer upon layer of government bureaucracy is simply not the answer, and no problem can ever be solved by just throwing money at it. Besides,... the answer seems to be much closer to home.

Personal Responsibility Is the Key

An in-depth Brookings Institute study concluded there are three basic things that, if we do them, all but guarantee we will avoid poverty. The study shows us the poverty rate could be substantially lowered by:

- Graduating high school
- Obtaining and keeping a full-time job
- Waiting to get married until after age twenty-one and not having children until after marriage

The study punctuates that for those who follow these guidelines, the odds of falling into poverty are less than 2 percent. In addition, they will have a 74 percent chance of being in the middle class or beyond. By contrast, those who violate all three recommendations have a 76 percent chance of ending up in poverty and only a 7 percent chance of making it into the middle class.

There are other factors that assist with upward mobility, such as having no more children than you can reasonably afford, abstaining from alcohol and drugs, and others.

> *"Poverty is not simply an economic issue; it is a behavioral issue, which is fueled by personal responsibility."*
> *—Brookings Institute*

The Brookings Institute study concluded, "Federal and state policymakers, program operators, teachers, and parents need to constantly remind themselves and their children that *personal responsibility is the key to success* and insist that children and adolescents demonstrate more of it. Without a relentless emphasis on personal responsibility, the billions of dollars we spend on government programs each year will continue to produce mediocre results and opportunity in America will continue to stagnate."

For too long, it has been promoted that the government should act as a caregiver to its citizens, and it is important to point out that no one ever led an excellent life by being dependent on others, especially the government. It is by relinquishing responsibility for ourselves to others that we become dependent, and, subsequently, fail to live up to our full potential. It is when we choose to allow others to have control over the seemingly small details of our lives that we lose the edge necessary to push through to a life of self-reliance, independence, and ultimately, freedom.

This is the hard and unvarnished fact: If we are to survive as a free people of a free and prosperous nation, it will be because we rely on *ourselves*, with God's guidance, to prosper within the freedoms granted through the government and not because we, in any way, depend on the government for anything other than to protect the freedoms, that we have been granted.

There are those who will say that America is no longer the land of opportunity or that the American Dream no longer exists, thus America has faltered or even failed. The plain and simple truth is that America has *not* failed; rather, its citizens, through our elected representatives, have failed America because we fail to protect her, and subsequently, fail to protect the freedoms and opportunities that exist for us all. Americans, and, indeed, anyone living in a free and civilized society should never rest on our freedoms, or those freedoms will be forever lost.

As a matter of protecting its citizens, the government can and should provide for those who cannot provide for themselves. Americans are, by nature, a caring and generous people, and we should all want to protect the most vulnerable among us. However, assistance should never be granted in a manner that would stifle the growth and future potential of those who receive it, or we risk the very foundation of the nation itself, as has been the case over the last half-century.

The United States will be, for the world, "the land of opportunity" only as long as we, as its citizens, act as caregivers to *her*, and do not take the opportunity she provides for granted or allow ourselves to fail to fully participate in it. Rest assured, the American Dream is alive and well for anyone, regardless of race, religion, sexual orientation, gender, or background who is willing to take it seriously, work hard, persist, and stake a claim. In a free society, upward mobility, a life of opportunity, and independence are the birthright of all those who have a dream for the future and are willing to persist to make the dream come true for themselves.

I would encourage you to go back and reread the chapters "Why We Struggle" and "Overcoming Our Circumstances." There is no doubt that life can be a challenge, but it is challenging for each of us in uniquely different ways. You will face challenges in your life unique to you, and it is up to you—and you alone—to muster the fortitude necessary to understand it and find the strength necessary to persevere through it.

There are many reasons for *when* and *why* we begin to take on the notion that we cannot achieve what we desire from life or that the American Dream is meant for others but not for ourselves. For those growing up in poverty and in poor neighborhoods, it is especially frustrating. The tendency for those who grow up in depressed surroundings is for their vision of what is possible to be depressed, as well.

For example, if you grow up in an affluent family and go to school with classmates who are also affluent, then all you see in your life and for your future is success and affluence. On the other hand, if you grow up in poverty and lack, then what you see for your future is poverty and lack. As a result, those growing up in depressed surroundings tend to take on the belief early in life that there is nothing to look forward to, nothing will ever change, and, therefore, there is nothing to work toward... And who can blame them?

So, what is the solution? With the millions upon millions of dollars spent to study the issue and the tens of trillions of dollars spent over a fifty-year period in an effort to solve it, the answer seems to have been uncovered by a young Black woman living in an inner-city neighborhood of Detroit with a third-grade education.

In the story of Sonya Carson, the genesis of her realization that she too could be lifted above her circumstances came through her noticing how her wealthy employers *thought* differently than she did. This planted a seed in her heart and mind that success in life was indeed possible and that it didn't seem to matter what a person's background was like. Later, she began to understand that these people were not that different from herself, and if they could live a life of prosperity, then she could too...

The very foundation of Sonya's belief that she could, through her own efforts and with God's help, raise herself and her two young boys out of poverty was seeing, through the lives of others, how it could be done. These subtle mentors were vital to her being able to secure the belief and faith necessary to know in her heart that *she* could do it, thus leading her to make the necessary changes—to take action.

*"What we fail to understand is that success is
less about talent and more about opportunity."*
—Malcolm Gladwell, Outliers

As discussed earlier, we tend to learn how to structure our lives through modeling the behavior of others. So, if the only examples we have of how to structure our lives are from those who are struggling themselves, then all we learn is how to struggle. For this reason, it is imperative that we model the behavior of those who have what we want and who have experienced and overcome similar conditions in life that we are facing or might face in the future. There is simply no other practical way for anyone, especially a kid who is growing up in the midst of poverty, to effectively navigate the challenges they will face and enter adulthood with the skills necessary to succeed.

What made it possible for Sonya to begin the process of pulling herself out of poverty was that she was subtly "mentored" by her employers. Maybe not in a direct or hands-on way, but rather in a subliminal or subconscious way. She was mentored while simply observing the *actions* and *behaviors* of those who had themselves been mentored and taught by others.

It was through observing how her employers lived their lives and interacted with their children that she was informally coached to learn to do the same thing for herself and her two young boys. What her employers did as a matter of natural habit, she was able to implement in a deliberate fashion for herself. The behaviors that her employers had grown accustomed to and implemented into their own lives and the lives of their children without conscious thought Sonja implemented into her life and the boys' lives in a very systematic and intentional way. This was for her, Curtis, and Ben the beginnings of the positive habits and positive character traits, that would be necessary for them to begin to move forward, out of their desperate situation.

It is often the smallest of changes that make the difference. It is the little seeds we plant in our hearts and minds, which, with time, germinate and grow to take our lives in a positive or negative direction. It is by being *intentional* and having a plan for how we approach even the smallest areas of our lives that we can build the positive habits necessary to ultimately find success.

The larger issue is for us to listen with our hearts and minds for where we are being guided and directed. For Ben Carson, the seed for him to become a doctor was planted when he was only eight years old. I have no doubt that when the notion of becoming a doctor first came into his mind, he didn't immediately list all the logical reasons why it could not be done. In the mind of a young child, anything is possible. It is only after we come in contact with others and the continual difficulties of life, that we begin the process of counting the obstacles in our path and convincing ourselves our dreams cannot be achieved.

It is as an infant who cannot imagine standing on its own two feet that we all begin our lives. If we knew ahead of time the obstacles and challenges we would face in our futures, how many of us would dare to stand and take that first step? But this is where we all begin. Unafraid to fail, unafraid to fall, and determined to get back up and persist, we instinctively and continually move forward. Unaware of what lies ahead, unaware that failure even exists, completely unaware and even uncaring of the trials we will face, we take our first step into a life of uncertainty. But as toddlers, we do this with joy in our hearts because we are proud of our accomplishments; we are excited to face the future, and we cannot wait to be challenged, tested, and grow.

As children, we are completely unaware of the larger understanding of what lies ahead in life, so we eagerly push on. But as life moves forward, we slowly become conscious of our perceived shortcomings and fears, thus becoming more tentative and cautious. At some point, we begin to compare ourselves to others and become more aware of how we, in our own minds, fall short. As we face more resistance, we can stop challenging ourselves and ultimately cease persisting. Why is this? For most, it is because we have a very limited understanding of what is possible for our lives, and we *learn* to avoid difficult and challenging situations. As a result, we tend to choose the path that involves less risk, less work, and where failure is less likely. We place far too much emphasis on short-term obstacles and count any setback as somehow final, insurmountable, or permanent.

The true tragedy in the lives of most is that we possess abilities far beyond what we believe possible, and we never put in the effort to uncover what God has placed deep within us to discover, thus robbing ourselves of our own future achievements and successes.

What Do We Have to Gain?

When generation after generation lives in poverty, when they see no way out and no hope for the future, what is going to turn the tide and reverse what seems to be an insurmountable and unfixable national and worldwide problem? Think for a minute what we, as a society, have to gain by taking the issue of poverty and lack of upward mobility seriously.

With increasing instances of drug abuse, drug-related incarcerations, violent crimes, fatherless homes, street riots, acts of terrorism, gang violence, decaying infrastructures, political upheavals, teen pregnancies, an overwhelming national debt, rising divorce rates, destroyed families, and attacks on the innocent, we have to ask, "Where is all of this headed?"

In the case of Sonja Carson, if it weren't for the examples set by others, she and her two sons were unlikely to have made it very far out of the streets of Detroit, and the world would have been robbed of the talents and abilities they possessed. This begs questions: How many other Curtis and Ben Carson's are there? How many thousands—or even tens of thousands—of our nation's children are giving up on their lives before they have even begun because they see little to no hope for their futures?

How many scientists, engineers, accountants, nurses, attorneys, mathematicians, scholars, pilots, entrepreneurs, schoolteachers, police officers, or doctors will never be realized because they gave up on those dreams before they ever had a chance? How many will remain in poverty because they never had anyone challenge them enough, teaching them to learn for themselves what talents and abilities God has placed within them to discover?

For any nation to prosper, it is necessary to make the best use of its resources, and the most important resource to any country is always within its people. A study by the Annie E. Casey Foundation states, "The bottom line is that if we don't get dramatically more children on track as proficient readers, the United States will lose a growing and essential proportion of its human capital to poverty, and the price will be paid not only by individual children and families but by the entire country."

For individuals—as well as for our nation—to prosper in the global economy and compete with the best and brightest the world has to offer, we must focus our attention and financial resources on improving and uplifting ourselves, as well as those around us, especially those in poverty and depressed circumstances.

Building the Bridge of Literacy

So, what does it take to alter a child's future? What does it take to lift them out of poverty and place them on the road to lives of options instead of obstacles? Too often, all it takes is for someone to whisper in their ear, "You can do it" and stick around long enough for them to believe it. Know that every child is just one caring adult away from the realization of the dreams in their heart.

"When we learn to read, we can learn how to do anything."
–Tomie dePaola

It is astonishing how many lives can be changed and improved by simply teaching a child how to read. It may seem overly simplistic or obvious that all children should be taught how to read, but the larger goal is that they are able to read *well* and can comprehend what they are reading.

Countless studies conclude that if a child learns to read at grade level by the first grade, but no later than the third grade, high school graduation and the road out of poverty are all but guaranteed. As the Brookings Institute study showed, for those who do not graduate from high school and who do not align their lives in a manner that predictably leads them toward achievement and upward mobility, then poverty, along with all of its associated negative consequences, is but a statistical certainty.

"Literacy is the bridge from misery to hope."
–Kofi Annan

Indeed, the pathway out of poverty, as well as to success later in life, begins while we are still in the laps of our parents. When a child learns to read, this opens up an entire world to them, one they may never otherwise know. For when we learn to read, we then have the ability to learn, and when we have the ability to learn, we can then take our lives in any positive direction we choose. Beyond this, education builds confidence and self-esteem and develops creativity and critical thinking abilities.

The Magic of Mentorship

A mentor is simply an experienced and trusted advisor. We need mentors to help us expand our vision of what is possible for our lives and our futures. They help us to see, in our own minds, what we are capable of achieving and give us the confidence and direction necessary to achieve those visions. We simply cannot accomplish this alone, thus the importance of having mentors in our lives cannot be overstated.

"One of the greatest values of mentors is the
ability to see ahead what others cannot see and to help
them navigate a course to their destination."
–John Maxwell

For those with quality mentors, there is an undeniable positive effect on the trajectory of a life. At every season, we need people in our lives to help, guide, and direct us so we can get on the right track and stay there. For most of us, we seldom fully appreciate how we have benefited from the subtle prodding and coaching we have received from the caring mentors in our lives.

Many of us tend to overlook the fact that we are born into close proximity to many experienced and trusted advisors, and we typically take the valuable lessons they offer for granted. These mentors might be our parents, grandparents, other relatives, teachers, coaches, or church leaders. It is important to know that in every season of life, we benefit from having people in our lives who have our best interests at heart, who can give relevant advice, and who continually whisper encouragement into our lives.

Make no mistake about it, at every age, we should have mentors in our lives. Warren Buffett mentored Bill Gates, Steve Jobs mentored Mark Zuckerberg, and every successful athlete or actor has had a coach. In fact, by the time an athlete makes it to the Olympic Games or any professional level, they are likely to have had dozens of coaches who helped them perfect their mental and physical performance. No one ever achieves success alone, and it is impossible for us to grow into our full potential without mentors. An excellent life demands it.

It is by opening up our lives to others through one-on-one, face-to-face mentoring that best solves the ills we face. One caring person sharing the wisdom, knowledge, and experiences of their life with another. Know that at every phase of life, it is through loving and patient mentoring that we can effectively alter and improve our lives.

You see, when children are raised in poverty or in depressed surroundings, they are seldom if ever, exposed to worthy and productive role models. If the only person they see in their lives that seems to be "successful" is a criminal or a drug dealer, we should not be surprised when they may one day become involved in crime and drugs. However, when a child is exposed to worthy role models through a systematic process of mentoring, this opens up an entirely new world.

When exposed to positive mentors who are educated and have achieved true and lasting success in their lives, children begin to see themselves and their futures in a completely different light. They begin to see through the lives of others that achievement and success are possible for them, as well. They begin to realize their background, race, religion, sexual orientation, or gender is not a determining factor in achieving success in life, and this ultimately alters their views of what is possible for them to accomplish.

While we may come into life with radically different backgrounds and with different perspectives, we have vastly more in common than we might realize. You see, we all want to be loved and treated with respect. We want to raise our families in peace and security. We want to worship God as we see fit, and we want to live our lives with honor, dignity, freedom, and prosperity. Simply put, for us to begin to solve the many ills we face and secure the American Dream for ourselves and for generations to come, we must open our minds, our hearts, and our arms.

Those who practice division must be replaced by those who seek acceptance and understanding. Those who want to pretend they are in some way superior to others of a different social or economic class need to count their blessings, thank God for what they have been given, roll up their shirt sleeves, and become involved in the lives of those who so desperately need to be shown the way up the ladder, out of poverty, and beyond. We simply cannot continue to allow our human capital to be squandered, lost to ignorance, complacency, and division.

God has blessed each of us with talents, abilities, and certain advantages, and it is up to us to use them—not in a selfish or self-serving way but to uplift and improve the lives of others. It is by our helping others, as well as others helping us that we all move forward.

It All Begins with a Dream

When a young child dreams of becoming a schoolteacher, doctor, engineer, or anything else, they need to know it is possible for their dream to be realized, and through an ongoing process of mentoring, it can be achieved. It is an inevitable consequence that when a person achieves success and fulfills their dream, they will then, by their positive example, inspire and launch the dreams of others, creating a domino effect of upward mobility.

One child at a time and one life at a time, we can alter the trajectory for the futures of individuals, families, neighborhoods, cities, our nation, and the world.

> *"Through hard work, perseverance, and faith in God, you can live your dreams."*
> *–Dr. Ben Carson*

If we are to live truly excellent lives, we cannot just sit back, watch the news, and mumble to ourselves that *someone* should do *something* about the negative events taking place before our very eyes. We can no longer afford to allow complacency and division to drive a wedge between us and stifle the growth and forward progress of our nation and its citizens.

For us to survive as a free and prosperous nation, we must once and for all, come together as a united and caring people. In America, it should not at all matter from where people come, what their gender is, what race or ethnicity they are, what sexual orientation they may be, the religion they practice, or anything else. To shun or discard others because of such things is to practice ignorance, and there is simply no place for it.

If we are able to live up to the ideals of our Founding Fathers—and indeed to the virtues God instilled in each of us—it will be because we have weaned ourselves off the sins of the past and look to the future with open minds and open hearts and treat one another the way we ourselves want to be treated.

If we are to continue to succeed as a nation and as a free and prosperous people, it will be because we have replaced *suspicion* with *acceptance* and *ignorance* with *understanding*, and in the process, find a way to work together to solve the issues we face.

If we, as a nation, are able to improve the future of those who struggle and, in the process, uplift ourselves by solving the most difficult issues we face, it will be because we individually and collectively care enough to take others by the hands, show them the correct path, and earnestly whisper into their ears, "You can do it!" This is indeed the path for us all to live truly excellent lives.

The Big Idea

- Choose to be self-reliant.
- Personal responsibility is essential to an excellent life.
- Discover the magic of mentorship.

Chapter 15
Givers and Takers

Life's most important and urgent question is,
what are you doing for others?
—Martin Luther King, Jr.

JAY calls his neighbor Bill to ask him if he can borrow his car.

"Hello, Bill. This is Jay. My car is in the shop for a few days. I know you have a spare, and I was curious if I could borrow it."

Jay grins and responds, "Sure, I am glad to help! Come on over, and I will have it ready for you."

A few minutes later, Jay knocks on Bill's door. "Hey, Bill, I really do appreciate you letting me borrow your car. I couldn't get to work without it. Plus, I have a lot of errands to take care of over the next couple of days, so this is a huge help."

"I'm glad to do it," replies Bill. "Here are the keys."

Jay gets behind the wheel and tells Bill he will take good care of the car. After starting the engine, Jay notices the car has just over three-quarters of a tank of gas and promises Bill he will fill the tank for him.

Bill responds, "That would be great," and waves good-bye as Jay pulls out of the driveway. A few miles down the road, Jay pulls into a gas station and tops off the tank.

Over the next two and a half days, Jay takes the car to and from work, runs his errands, and drives almost 275 miles. After picking his own car up from the repair shop, Jay takes the borrowed car back to Bill.

"Hey, Bill, I sure do appreciate you letting me borrow the car. It was a real life-saver!"

Bill, genuinely glad to have been able to help, assures his friend that he can borrow the car anytime. They talk a little more, and then Bill waves goodbye.

A couple of hours later, Bill decides to take the car that Jay had borrowed for a drive. Bill immediately notices that the car has less than a quarter tank of gas. Remembering that Jay had promised to fill the tank, Bill decides to call Jay. "Hey, Jay, this is Bill. I was just curious if you forgot your promise to fill the gas tank."

"No," Jay replies. "I filled the tank just like I said I would."

Bewildered, Bill responds, "Well then, why does the car have less than a quarter tank of gas?"

Jay responds defensively, "Well, I told you that I filled the gas tank. Are you calling me a liar?"

What happened here? Did Jay indeed fulfill his promise to Bill? Was Bill wrong to have questioned Jay? While Jay did fill the gas tank, was it fair of Bill to assume that Jay's promise should have been carried out *after* he had driven 275 miles instead of before? This is an example of the classic "giver" and "taker" personalities and how some will let no good deed go unpunished.

How about you? Are you a *giver* or a *taker*? Are you the person who holds the door for someone else, or are you the one who cuts others off in traffic? Of course, no one is a giver or a taker all the time. There are times when givers take and times when takers give. But the vast majority of us instinctively lean in one direction or the other. Some are *selfless* while others are more *self-centered*. We all know people who are true givers as well as people who instinctively seek to gain personal benefits through the kindness and generosity of others.

What we are discussing here are the basic motivations, strengths, and weaknesses we all share as human beings. Ralph Waldo Emerson wrote, "To have a friend, you have to be one," and it is difficult, if not impossible, to be a real friend without being a giver. To live a truly excellent life, it is essential to develop a heart for giving, as well as to surround yourself with givers. For those who are true givers, there is almost nothing more uplifting than the feeling of satisfaction that comes from helping another person. As St. Francis of Assisi said, "For it is in giving that we receive."

I want to take a moment to outline the fundamental underlying differences between givers and takers so there is a clear understanding of the psychology of each, thus highlighting the effect of each on and in our lives.

The Anatomy of Givers and Takers

The giver asks, "How can I help," while the taker asks, "What's in it for me?"

The giver seeks to improve the lives of those around them, while the taker seeks to have those around them serve their own needs.

Givers understand that serving others gives life meaning and purpose, while taking from others leads to a life of expectation and entitlement.

Givers are honest in their dealings with others, while takers tend to rationalize why their deception is justified.

The giver gives with compassion and kindness, while the taker tends to see compassion and kindness as a weakness to be exploited.

The giver is *dependable* while the taker is *dependent*.

The giver accepts responsibility for their own actions and behavior, while the taker projects responsibility and blame onto others for their own shortcomings, inadequacies, or failures.

Givers are trusting and typically offer friendship and love unconditionally, while takers are suspicious and offer friendship and love with conditions.

The giver grasps that a quality, healthy relationship requires giving of themselves, while the taker continually keeps score of who did what for whom and often complains about feeling slighted.

The giver has learned the secrets of contentment, while the taker seeks gratification through possessions and controlling others.

The giver goes out of their way to help others, while the taker says, "I'm too busy."

The giver is driven by love, while the taker is driven by self-interests.

Givers inject energy, vitality, and enthusiasm, while takers drain the life out of those around them.

The giver submits and humbles themselves to leadership, while the taker is resentful, divisive, and suspicious.

The giver serves in the background, willingly and unconditionally, while the taker seeks attention, reward, and recognition.

Relationships Between Givers and Takers

Two Takers

This is typically a very short relationship. In any relationship where there are two takers, neither is fulfilled because there is virtually nothing for them to take from the other. Both are looking to be served by someone else, so they easily feel imposed upon and quickly feel unsatisfied, frustrated, or taken advantage of. When this occurs, they usually just move on to seek out a more fulfilling opportunity.

A Giver and a Taker

There are a lot of complexities that can develop within this type of relationship, but the end result is typically sifted down to just two very predictable and probable ends.

The first result is that at some point in the relationship, the giver begins to feel bewildered, isolated, and confused. The giver often believes the relationship is unsatisfying or has conflict because of their own shortcomings. The giver, concerned that maybe they didn't give enough, doubles and re-doubles their effort in giving, completely unaware that the more they give, the more disappointed, disillusioned, and dismayed they will ultimately become.

The second result is that the giver will simply continue to give until there is nothing left for the taker to take. This can and often does leave the giver completely broken financially, emotionally, and spiritually. When this happens, the taker simply blames the giver, saying, "You don't make me happy anymore" and moves on to seek out someone else who they think can make them happy, and the cycle continues.

Two Givers

The Bible speaks of two people being "equally yoked," and this is an important part of that. Two givers simply cannot "out give" one another. They understand that a healthy and productive relationship must consist of two people giving completely of themselves to one another. They give to each other without expectation of reciprocation. They give with absolute openness, honesty, trust, and love. They give to the other without jealousy, envy, or pride.

There are few areas of our lives that we can contribute more to living an excellent life than when one truly giving person shares their life with another giver.

I quoted Emerson earlier and will do so again here: "It is one of the beautiful compensations in this life that no one can sincerely try to help another without helping himself."

Conclusion

Proverbs 28:27 says, "Whoever gives to the poor will not want, but he who hides his eyes will get many a curse." Being a true giver is simply a way of expressing love and grace to others. Giving and caring for others can only be expressed by our actions, and this is done through the heart. Becoming a giver and building a heart for giving is accomplished by deliberately seeking out those whom you can give to and looking for opportunities and ways to help and be of service to others. Authentic giving is accomplished when you give to someone who cannot do anything for you in return.

Do you consider yourself a *giver*? Maybe? Maybe not…? This can certainly be one of those areas where we may not be the best judge. Either way, let me challenge you to do this… As you go about your daily life, look for ways you can help others. The next time you are walking into a store, hold the door open for the person behind you, especially if they are several steps behind you. Just open the door and stand there allowing them to walk in ahead of you. When you pass a stranger, put on a warm smile, make eye contact, and simply say, *Hello*. When you are at the grocery store, look for someone to help by returning their shopping cart. Instead of walking past that bit of trash in the parking lot, stop and pick it up. When you see someone struggling with a heavy load, offer to help them.

Make a point to take notice of those whom you drive past every day, the ones who walk the streets because they have nowhere else to be and no home or job to go to. I challenge you to keep a couple of bottles of water, some protein bars, or a pack of crackers in your car to pass out when you see these individuals. When it is cold outside, have an extra jacket or blanket in the car to give away.

Take the time to say hello, look them in the eyes, shake their hands, or pat them on the back, and feel their sincere appreciation as you hand them that bottle of water, a snack, or a warm blanket. Notice how they respond. Feel the pain they may release as you give them the small gifts, as they see and experience your love and compassion.

I challenge you to serve a meal at a homeless shelter, visit or write a letter to someone in prison, help a young child learn to read, or volunteer your time whenever and wherever you can. Make a point to intentionally and deliberately look for those in your city to whom you can help and be of service. Don't just donate your money but roll up your sleeves and give them your time, your heart, your love, and your sincere prayers.

What does this cost you? Almost nothing. And what does it mean to them? There is no telling how you might have helped them. In many cases, this goes well beyond the physical aspect of a drink of water, a bite to eat, or a warm blanket. To some, your small kindness might represent their last bit of *hope or* could be their first small step in knowing that someone cared enough to notice them, signifying, "I care about you and you have value."

Those who truly and unconditionally give to others are blessed themselves because they are building a heart that is free from coveting, envy, jealousy, greed, and pride, and in its place, their hearts are becoming filled with compassion, empathy, love, and grace.

Developing a heart for giving puts the giver on a path that expands and builds their character in endless and countless ways. And as a result, they are ultimately blessed with lasting, caring, loving, and truly meaningful relationships, which can last a lifetime. Those who have a true heart for giving will receive rewards and blessings they won't expect, cannot foresee, and simply cannot imagine.

On the other hand, understand that giving with strings attached or with insincere motives is not really giving at all and is actually just a way of *taking* in disguise. To give to someone but to have ulterior motives in your heart is merely a form of manipulation that can be harmful and is nothing more than a way of controlling others.

There are also cases where people can give to the point of co-dependency, creating an excessive emotional or psychological reliance on others, which is certainly unhealthy and counterproductive. Always be mindful of this, and if you find yourself leaning in this direction, seek the guidance of those who have expertise in this area.

We are all called upon to be givers and not to question the motives of others. I am sure God is perfectly capable of sorting it all out when the time comes. We are all called upon to love each other in every way possible. However, there are simply times when we have to be strong enough and wise enough to know when and how to separate ourselves from people in our lives who have selfish, insincere, or destructive motives, which could cause real harm to us or those around us.

Know that there is nothing more important or more rewarding in this life than sincerely and cheerfully helping, giving, and being of service to others. Being a true giver and giving of yourself to others is one of the many foundational and mandatory aspects of building *and living* an excellent life.

The Big Idea

- Build a heart of giving.
- Always be mindful of our tendencies to *take* from others.
- Show kindness to those in need.

Chapter 16
Heroes versus Celebrities

"Time makes heroes, but dissolves celebrities."
–Daniel J. Boorstin

I HAVE an enormous amount of respect for anyone who places their personal safety or life on the line for others. Soldiers, law enforcement officers, firefighters, emergency service personnel, you name it. The contributions made by these selfless people on a daily basis to *protect and serve* their fellow man are truly unimaginable, and the debt we owe them can never be fully repaid.

Webster's Dictionary defines a *hero* as "a person of distinguished courage or ability, admired for their brave deeds and noble qualities" or "a person who in the opinion of others has performed a heroic act and is regarded as model or ideal."

Think about the men and women who have not just risked their lives for each and every one of us but, in many cases, have actually *given* their lives. Think about the sacrifices they have made, what they risked, what they must do without, and what they have left behind. Think about their courage and where that courage comes from. Think about their families and what they are asked to endure. Think about all of it. Would you trade places with them?... Could you?

In fighting the wars in Iraq and Afghanistan, 7,057 American soldiers were killed in action. The Law Enforcement Memorial Fund in Washington, D.C., honors the nearly 21,000 officers who lost their lives in the line of duty to protect and serve Americans, and sadly, this number continues to grow. Over the past ten years, there have been 1,627 law enforcement officers who have died in the line of duty, which is an astonishing one every fifty-four hours. Firefighters die in the line of duty at an average rate of 126 per year. They all know the risks when they sign on for duty, and for this reason, they are indeed *heroes!* The courageous men and women who serve our nation and our communities so selflessly are all heroes, and they deserve our gratitude, our most sincere admiration, and our deepest respect.

A *celebrity*, as defined by *Webster's*, is "a person in popular culture who has a prominent profile and commands a great degree of public fascination and influence in day-to-day media." Wikipedia adds, "someone may gain celebrity status as a result of a successful career in a particular field, primarily in the areas pertaining to sports and entertainment. In other cases, people become celebrities due to media attention for their extravagant lifestyle or wealth..."

The reason I go to such lengths to detail these definitions is that there seems to be a blending in our society of *heroes* and *celebrities*. How does it happen that a celebrity can be confused with a hero? I can certainly understand that when we watch the Olympics or a college or professional ballgame and see these magnificent athletes perform as they do, that it may seem heroic, but in actuality, it is not. I can see where a sportscaster, in an attempt to add drama to a game, may misuse the term and refer to an athlete as a hero, but, in fact, the term, *is* being misused.

I am a huge sports fan, and as a former athlete, I am fully aware of what it takes to compete at that level. Professional, college, and Olympic athletes make what they do seem almost easy when it is anything but. But again, they are far from being heroes.

I believe the casual misuse of the term *hero* does a great injustice to and, in effect, waters down legitimate heroism. It also unduly uplifts the celebrity, or "synthetic hero" to an unearned level of admiration. It is important to understand that there is an enormous difference between someone who risks their very life to save another and someone who performs the same act in a movie or excels on the athletic field, and yet somehow, it tends to be viewed as one and the same.

I love movies. Going to the movies is a common ritual for my wife and me. It is among my favorite ways to relax and set aside the stresses of life. There are many people who can sit for hours and name all of their favorite celebrities. They can discuss the roles they've played in their most recent television shows or movies. Many can name every single major sports franchise, as well as the starting quarterback for every National Football League team. I know people who can tell you the batting average of every single player on their favorite Major League Baseball team. Some can talk for hours about the winners of the most popular national talent shows or the exploits of the latest "celebrity gone wild" or the intimate details of the most recent reality show star.

I admire and am certainly in awe of the time and talent it takes to produce a movie or television show. And while the behavior of the character the actor is playing on-screen may be heroic, the actor should not be viewed as a hero simply because they play the role of one. Similarly, those who donate money or speak out for a cause, no matter how worthy, should never be elevated beyond the status of a kind and caring individual.

Don't get me wrong, we should all be thankful for those of means who, with compassion and generosity, unselfishly give to charities or donate their money to worthy causes. However, those who give out of their abundance should in no way be elevated to the status of a hero. After all, no one ever risked their lives or even faced personal risk by writing a check, no matter how large.

Okay. So, what is the point? The point is that, to date, America has awarded 3,511 different men and one woman the Congressional Medal of Honor, and nineteen of them have received the award twice. But can you name even *one* of these actual heroes? At the time of this writing, there have been eighteen Medals of Honor awarded to those engaged in the wars in Iraq and Afghanistan, and there will be more to come. Do you know the real-life stories of any of these unimaginably brave, *actual heroes?* What do you know about their unselfish courage or what they did to receive such an honor?

What do you know about the heroic bayonet charge led by Colonel Joshua Chamberlain on Little Round Top at Gettysburg? Do you know the story of "the lost battalion" and how Captain Charles Whittlesey and his men held their positions and heroically fought on though they had been given up for dead in the Argonne Forest of France in the final days of World War I? Do you know anything about Sergeant John Basilone and how he almost single-handedly held off a relentless and overwhelming suicide charge of some 3,000 Japanese troops *after* his fifteen-man platoon was reduced to just two men at Guadalcanal? What do you know about any of the 136 Medal of Honor recipients from Korea or the 248 from Vietnam?

What do you know about the fifty-six unimaginably brave men who signed our Declaration of Independence? By signing their names on this great document, these men were literally signing their own death warrants. Outside of a famous few, do you know their stories? Do you have any idea what they risked, sacrificed, or fought for so we could have our freedom and live the lives that we take for granted each and every day?

Did you know there were 411 first responders who died in the terrorist attacks on the World Trade Centers on September 11, 2001? They were NYC firefighters, NYC police officers, Port Authority police officers, and private EMS and paramedics. These are the brave men and women who were running *into* the ill-fated buildings as everyone else was desperately attempting to run *out*. Can you name any of them? Can you name even one law enforcement officer, firefighter, or EMT in your community?

Today, our nation's police officers, who are sworn to "protect and serve" each and every one of us, regardless of race, religion, gender, social status, level of income, or political view, are being hunted down, ambushed, and assassinated in the streets of America. With very limited exceptions, these men and women perform honorably, bravely, and heroically as a matter of routine, and yet, most of us have no idea who they are. Not only do they receive little to no real reward or recognition, but they are also viewed by some with suspicion, resentment, and even condemnation. I challenge you to trade places with them and walk in their shoes. Most would not do so for even a day, and very few outside their ranks would be up to the challenge.

Why is it that we, as a society, tend to downplay actual heroism yet celebrate the actors who play the role of imaginary or fictitious heroes? Why is it that we so often idolize and even worship the great athletes and actors of our time when we seem to hardly even notice the actual heroes among us? Why is a *celebrity* so celebrated?

It is certainly understandable that we might find ourselves in awe of the level of talent and abilities of an athlete or actor. It is understandable that we may highly admire, look up to, and greatly respect those with such talent, but what they do and the way we revere them does not make them heroes. We should all take great care in who we choose to raise up and exalt and what behaviors and traits we choose to aspire to, emulate, envy, or idolize.

Understand that an excellent life is a life of gratitude, of being thankful for those who so completely, quietly, and unselfishly give of themselves. I would call on us all to do our very best to seek out the actual heroes who live among us. I challenge you to get to know the law enforcement officers, firefighters, military personnel, and EMS who serve your community. I call on you to pray for them and ask God to help, guide, and protect them. Do your best to recognize and uplift these brave men and women who so selflessly and honorably serve us all. When you see them in your community, introduce yourself, shake their hands, and tell them how much you appreciate their service. Show your gratitude for what they do for each and every one of us. Introduce your kids to them and learn their stories, contribute to their causes, and support their charities. And then, with that done, maybe you can go to a movie or maybe a ballgame.

The Big Idea

- There is an enormous difference between a *celebrity* and a *hero*.
- Learn about those who sacrificed everything for your freedoms.
- Show gratitude for those who gave it all for you.

Chapter 17
Go Ahead, Sweat the Small Stuff

"Change things that can be changed, accept those that cannot, and have the wisdom to know the difference."
—Richard Carlson

I REALLY like Richard Carlson's *Don't Sweat the Small Stuff.* This insightful book points out simple ways for us to "slow down and calm down" so we can keep all the little things that drive us crazy from taking over our lives. If you haven't read it, I do recommend that you pick up a copy. But for our purpose here, I am going to encourage you to absolutely "sweat the small stuff," knowing that our character and our integrity are formed by intentionally and deliberately building one small positive act, one atop of another.

"A small leak can sink a great ship."
—Benjamin Franklin

I had lunch one afternoon with some friends at an upscale sports bar. It was like a fine dining restaurant with dimmed lights and tablecloths but outfitted with several televisions and vintage pool tables. Just as we were seated, I noticed a man in a white lab coat walking across the restaurant floor with a large black leather case. He placed the case down beside an elaborately carved but worn and tattered mahogany pool table about ten feet from where we were seated. It was a curious sight to see. It seemed as if he was a surgeon, preparing to operate on a billiards table, and it didn't take long to figure out that this was exactly what he was going to do.

I had never seen anyone re-felt a pool table and judging by the way this guy was approaching his work, I knew we were in for a special treat. I don't know where he learned his craft, but I am confident that I have never seen anyone approach their work with more professionalism, skill, and attention to even the smallest of details. He was part surgeon and part artist as he flawlessly shifted from one phase of the job to the next without a misplaced hand. It was a sight to behold as he worked with his tools, removing and replacing the bumpers and felt with precision and confidence. Around and around the table he worked, never second-guessing, never hesitating as he almost magically transformed the worn table into a renewed creation of his own design.

The new, dark wool felt had a sheen to it that glistened with approval as he rolled the balls across the length and width of the table. The thumping of the bumpers was like music as he tested and retested his new masterpiece. He then went around the table with a small level, checking every inch of the table to ensure it was in perfect balance. Next, he went back to his black bag and took out some wax and a cloth. He painstakingly massaged the wax into every nook and cranny of the elaborately carved wood. He took his time to buff and re-buff the rich wood to a deep, mirror-like luster that almost seemed to glow.

As he completed his work, he circled the table, again and again, his eyes steadfast as he searched every inch of the table for even the slightest flaw or imperfection. I almost expected applause to erupt from the patrons as he completed his performance; it really was a pleasure to watch.

With his work seemingly complete, the restaurant owner approached him with a wide grin and a check in hand. As they finalized the paperwork, the owner looked at the table with pride as he admired the beautiful work. He then shook the man's hand and retreated to the kitchen.

Just before leaving, the "surgeon" pulled one last item out of his bag. It was the dot typically placed where the balls are racked on the table. I halfway expected him to pull out some elaborate measuring device or an ancient brass compass to divinely measure, down to the last atom, the proper spot for the dot. But that's not what he did. He just placed the dot, grabbed his large black leather bag. and promptly left the restaurant.

As he was leaving, he passed two young men who walked straight to the newly completed masterpiece. As they racked the balls, one of the guys had an odd look on his face. I expected him to remark about how beautiful the new felt looked and how well-balanced the table was or how the elaborately carved wood glowed. I just knew he was going to express his admiration for the artistry, which had been performed just minutes prior to his arrival.

But that is not what he did. Instead, he exclaimed, "what moron did this?" pointing to the dot on the table. As he spoke, I couldn't help but look for myself. Sure enough, the dot was out of position by nearly an inch to one side. Unbelievable! I just stood there with my mouth hanging open as the two men joked that whoever put the dot on the table should never be allowed to touch a pool table again. How could it be that this lab-coat-wearing, black-medical-bag-toting "surgeon" could make such an error in placing the dot? The job he performed on the pool table, transforming it from tattered and worn to a work of art, was unquestionably meticulous. So, what happened here?

It's easy. He didn't sweat the smallest part of his job. In fact, he took it for granted.

Just how do you think the restaurant owner reacted when he saw the dot? Well, I can tell you because just as the two men were commenting about the misplaced dot, the owner happened to walk by. He stood there, just as I had done, with his mouth hanging open in disbelief. The dot remained misplaced for years.

Do you think the restaurant owner ever called the "surgeon" in the lab coat back to update another table? I think not. Do you think the "surgeon" ever wondered why he didn't do any more work for the restaurant? Who knows?

I always considered this experience to be a valuable life lesson. I have noticed time and time again, it seems to be the smallest of things that tend to set us back or cause us the biggest problems in life, and we seldom, if ever, realize it.

The small things in life absolutely matter because they lead to larger and more substantial things. Testing us with the small and seemingly insignificant is life's way of preparing us for the much larger future that we have in store for us.

It's the tiny "white lie" that leads to bigger lies. It is the small lapses of integrity that lead to larger ones. We begin with the smallest fragments of a negative habit, and they can eventually consume, bind, and control us. As Og Mandino points out in his classic book, *The Greatest Salesman in the World*, "Our habits are like cobwebs that turn into cables to either straighten or shackle our lives."

You see, when we have an inspiration or thought that in some way leads to our doing something that we know to be wrong, if we don't correct ourselves and, where appropriate, seek forgiveness, it becomes perpetually easier to do it again in the future, until it eventually builds into a negative and destructive habit. When Mandino says our habits are like "cobwebs," he is communicating that in the beginning, they are nothing more than flimsy notions or thoughts and are almost undetectable or unnoticeable, seeming to have little substance, much like a cobweb. But when we *act* on them and repeat these actions over and over again, the choices and actions gradually take on greater substance and eventually form into negative and destructive habits. The negative habits, with repetition and over time, are spun into something much more substantial and seemingly unbreakable, like steel cables, which can shackle and imprison us. So, over time and without corrective action, what was once seemingly small and flimsy can grow more substantial and ultimately bind us to where we cannot overcome it without great and sustained effort.

It is important to realize that the reverse is also true. As Mandino says, the same process that can "shackle" our life can also "straighten" it and give our life meaning and substance. We can indeed use this same process to strengthen and reinforce our positive habits, which build our characters and our futures. Positive and constructive habits are the key to greatness and a life of passion, freedom, and wholeness. As the nineteenth-century writer George Eliot once penned, "Great things are not done by impulse, but by a series of small things brought together."

What Eliot is telling us is that great character, true integrity, and excellent lives are formed intentionally and deliberately by paying close attention to the small and seemingly insignificant circumstances of our lives. For this reason, there can often be a thin line between living a life of anxiety, worry, fear, and frustration and the life-altering freedom that comes from intentionally living a life of integrity, strong character, and excellence. The good news is that this is in our own hands and one hundred percent up to us.

Don't misunderstand me. I'm not telling you to *worry* about the small things in life; I'm telling you to work to master them. I'm not telling you to let the little things control you; I'm telling you to take action and be in control. I'm not telling you to stress over the small and the meaningless; I'm telling you to strive to live an excellent life that has meaning, integrity, and is based on positive character and time-tested virtues.

Understand that success or failure in life is *absolutely* dictated by a series of seemingly small and insignificant choices built one atop another. This process is up to you because only *you* can decide who you are, the kind of person you want to become, and the life you will ultimately lead.

No one can decide your fate for you. Like it or not, the decisions you are faced with day in and day out and the choices you make in your life place you in total and complete control of yourself and your future.

So the choice is completely yours... You can live a life filled with *excuses* and *regrets*, or you can choose a life of *no* excuses and *no* regrets... Your future is in your own hands.

The Big Idea

- Build positive habits.
- Take care of or improve the small things because they matter.
- Small choices and habits combine to influence your character and success.

Chapter 18

Money

"Winning with money is 80 percent behavior
and 20 percent head knowledge."
–Dave Ramsey

THE most important takeaway from this book might be that worthwhile goals cannot be consistently and predictably achieved without being very intentional concerning your approach to the most important areas of your life, and this is certainly true in dealing with money. So here it is… Having a proper and correct view of money and understanding how money fits into your life could be *the* determining factor in your being able to achieve, maintain, and to live an excellent life, so let's get this right.

I think it must be acknowledged that having money is important—in some cases, vitally important—but the role that we *allow* money to play in our lives needs to be carefully considered, thought through, and understood.

The subject of money is such an important and complicated topic that it has proven to be, by far, the most difficult for me to write about. I am sure that many of you may wonder why the topic of money could be so difficult. After all, money is money, and we all know what it is and what it is for. I mean, we use money to buy what we want and what we need. So what is complicated about that? Well, the last sentence exposes the foundation of the issue. There is what we *want*, and there is what we *need*, and we can spend our entire lives never truly grasping the difference between the two.

A *want* is merely something we have a desire for. We want a new car, we want a nice home, we want a new "toy," and we want to have nice things. A *need*, on the other hand, is something *essential*, something we cannot reasonably do without. So, if the difference between what we *want* and what we *need* is so obvious, then why is this topic so complicated? Frankly, it is complicated because we make it complicated. We do this by convincing ourselves that something that is not essential actually is.

Please don't misunderstand. I am not telling you that you shouldn't want or have nice things. I mean, I think everyone likes to have nice things—I know I do. I don't think there is anyone who hasn't daydreamed at some point about what it would be like to be "rich." There is just something about the thought of living in a big, expensive house, driving the finest cars, or jetting around the world. We see celebrities, artists, and sports stars who seem to have life in the palm of their hands, and we, in some cases, elevate them to the highest status in society.

Let me ask you a question. If you took thirty minutes to write down all the different things that you *want*, how long would the list be? Ten items long? Fifty items? A hundred things or more? And yet, it shouldn't take but a minute for you to whittle it down to the foundational things you actually *need*, those being the basics of food, shelter, clothing, and transportation. This begs the question: If our actual needs are so basic, then why do we have so much *stuff*?

So, what's going on here? It doesn't take much research to learn that the average person has a debt problem. And, interestingly, it doesn't seem to matter how much we make. Higher incomes oddly seem only to translate into being in debt at a much higher level.

I'm not going to bore you with all the statistics on debt, but for most, being in debt and staying in debt is simply a way of life. It seems as though having a large mortgage, multiple car payments, and credit card debt is just the way "*it*" is done.

Why do we feel so compelled to buy a home larger than we need? Why do we buy a car that we have to go into debt to own? Why do we use credit cards as if the bill is not going to come in the mail each month? And on top of that, it is shocking how little we *save*.

Am I hitting a nerve here? If not, I congratulate you because you are in the great minority. Understand that the purpose here is not to merely point out that we spend too much on things we don't actually need or that we *save* too little. The larger question is *why* we do these things; and, how we can turn this around?

I think it is important at this point to take a step back and take a hard look at what the goal is: being able to live *an excellent life*. We discussed in the chapter titled "Self-Awareness and Self-Observation" that it is impossible to live an excellent life without achieving *balance* in the seven important areas of our lives, and none of these are more important than *money*.

Just think for a minute about how important money and finances are in our lives. There is certainly more to money than the physical reality of having or not having money in the bank. Having our finances in order can change our lives for the better in many important ways. Being financially independent can decrease stress, pay off your home, pay for an education, restore health, allow you to help those in need, and so many other positive things. To the contrary, incorrect handling of money can end relationships, destroy families, and absolutely ruin lives. In fact, there are few things in our lives that can do so much good and yet be so completely destructive.

Why is it that money can be so essential to building a positive, healthy, and productive life to some and yet be so catastrophic to others? Why does the steady accumulation of money and wealth seem to come so easily for some, and yet, for others, it is totally elusive? Or, equally troubling are the potential unintended consequences of having so much money that it causes a deterioration of values, which can lead to destructive actions.

Exactly what are the qualities of *character* that can move our lives forward and give us the ability to eliminate debt, achieve financial success, and accumulate wealth, or when we do have wealth, keep us on track? They are the traits of honesty, compassion, empathy, loyalty, generosity, thrift, dedication, patience, and outstanding work ethic, among others. Understand that it is these positive traits of character, combined with continual *self-discipline,* that give us the ability to achieve meaningful, long-term goals.

If we take a close look at what it means to be *self-disciplined,* we learn its relationship to being focused, organized, persistent, responsible, and resilient. People who are self-disciplined set goals; they develop positive habits, set boundaries for themselves, are highly motivated, and are driven by logic—not by emotion, greed, or fear. They do not allow themselves to give in to temptations, which can move their lives in the wrong direction. They stay the course and understand that anything of true and lasting value is developed over time and with relentless patience.

> *"Money often costs too much."*
> *–Ralph Waldo Emerson*

One issue can be in how we view those who are wealthy. What do you think of when you consider those who are in the "millionaire class?" Do you believe that *you* can join the ranks of the financially independent? I find it interesting when I talk with people about those who are considered wealthy. There seems to be a troubling false assumption or belief that those who are wealthy have accumulated their wealth because of luck, inheritance, or even dishonesty. Know that nothing could be farther from the truth, and a close study of those who have accumulated a high net worth reveal some interesting statistics.

Chris Hogan, in his best-selling book *Everyday Millionaires,* after surveying and studying over 10,000 millionaires, reveals that 80% of them are self-made; they come from families who were at or below middle-class status, and they built their wealth through hard work, avoiding debt, being self-reliant, disciplined, and responsible.

Indeed, the evidence is clear that vastly more wealth is being created by very ordinary people with a regular paycheck and a dose of good ole fashioned hard work and self-discipline than through any other way.

In his book, Hogan deals with some common myths and misconceptions about the wealthy, so let's learn the facts:

Myth # 1: "Wealthy people *inherited* their money." Suggesting they got wealthy because it was given to them and not earned.

Truth: "79% of millionaires received *no* inheritance, meaning that only 21% received any inheritance at all. Sadly, 74% of millennials and 52% of baby boomers believe millionaires inherited *all* of their wealth."

Myth # 2: "Wealthy people are just lucky." Suggesting they were born with an unusual talent or ability such as a professional athlete or celebrity, or their wealth came through some risky scheme or the lottery.

Truth: "76% of millionaires earned their wealth through discipline and hard work." The fact is that millionaires are savers… "70% of millionaires saved more than 10% of their income throughout their working years."

Myth # 3: "Wealthy people make risky investments." Implying some type of special investment knowledge unavailable to the "average" wage earner.

Truth: "79% of millionaires reached millionaire status through their employer-sponsored retirement plan." In fact, the number one contributing factor to millionaires' high net worth is in investing in retirement plans.

Myth # 4: "Wealthy people take stupid risks to get rich quick." Some falsely believe that if someone is "rich," it is because they cheated others or won the money in Vegas.

Truth: "The average millionaire hits the $1 million mark at 49 years old. This is after years, even decades of hard work. Only 5% of millionaires got there in ten years or less." Plus "92% of millionaires develop a long-term plan for their money, compared with 60% of the general population."

Myth # 5: "Wealthy people have prestigious private school educations." Suggesting that for someone to reach millionaire status, they must have had a privileged upbringing.

Truth: "79% of millionaires did not attend prestigious private schools. 62% graduated from public state colleges or universities, 8% attended community college, and 9% never graduated college at all."

One surprising fact Hogan points out is that when millionaires were asked the question. "Do you believe that you are in control of your own destiny?" (as it relates to money, as well as other major "life" issues) "an astonishing 97% agreed that they were, while for the general public, only 54% agreed with this statement."

Why is it that so many falsely believe they are not in the driver's seat when it comes to breaking out of the middle class and into the millionaire class, or that debt will always be their reality? Far too many believe it doesn't matter how hard they work or how hard they try; they will always struggle financially.

> *"Financial success is not a hard science. It is a soft skill, where your behavior is more important than what you know."*
> *–Morgan Housel*

Why is it that so many fail to accumulate wealth and remain in debt? There is a multitude of reasons for this... Many do not succeed financially because they simply do not want to make the necessary sacrifices. They want to keep up appearances or just enjoy buying "stuff," not realizing how they are sabotaging their futures.

Understand that dealing with money, finances, and debt is something that everyone must figure out and learn at some point, and nearly everyone makes mistakes. No one dances out of the womb with the experience, wisdom, and knowledge it takes to succeed with money, and even the best advisors on this topic have had to learn this the hard way.

To me, the clear authority on the subject of having the correct perspective as it relates to money is Dave Ramsey. Dave intimately understands the *"logic"* and *"emotional"* aspects of money, having become a millionaire in his 20s, only to lose it all, learn hard lessons, and rebuild. He is very open and disarmingly candid in telling his story. For over 30 years, Dave Ramsey (through his company Ramsey Solutions) has helped millions of people get out of debt and turn their financial lives around. I highly encourage you to look into what he teaches.

The bottom line concerning money is that being financially independent is about creating a life of freedom and avoiding the bondage of debt.

Know that learning to achieve balance in your life as it relates to money is an acquired skill that must be developed. This is a mandatory and completely unavoidable component in your quest to live an excellent life.

The Big Idea

- Financial success is a result of building character and self-discipline.
- Understand the difference between wants and needs.
- No failure is permanent unless we quit.

Chapter 19
Turning Thoughts and Ideas into Action

"In order to succeed, your desire for success must
be greater than your fear of failure."
–Albert Einstein

A **CLOSE** friend of mine is always telling me about the great ideas he
has for starting endless different businesses. It seems he always has
an innovative idea for some new product or invention. He has, without a
doubt, one of the most creative minds I have ever encountered, but there
is only one problem, he never actually *does* any of it!

Oh, he can tell you a thousand different ways to make a fortune, and he
can tell you all about his latest and greatest plans. But all of them remain
locked away in his mind where they are destined to stay; that is until
someone else actually does it.

Does this sound like anyone you know? I'll bet it does. They are the people
who continually talk about the things they are going to do "someday" or
the things they are going to do "when." These ideas could be something
as simple as a trip they want to take but never go on or a project they
want to start but the timing is just never quite right.

The Process of Getting Things Done

Have you ever thought about the difference between someone who
continually wishes for something and someone who actually follows
through and gets it done? What is the difference between someone who

forever dreams of accomplishing a goal or an important task and someone who actually follows through on their ideas?

We all have things we want to accomplish or achieve in our lives, but most people seem to get stuck somewhere between having the thought or idea of what they want to do and actually following through and getting it done.

There is a ten-step logistical process each of us goes through to carry something from a simple *inspiration* or *thought*, all the way to its final completion, which is as follows:

1. An *inspiration* or *thought* enters our minds. This is typically nothing more than a fleeting or passing notion, which in itself has little substance.
2. The inspiration or thought, when focused on, dwelled upon, or shared with others, gradually gains form and turns into an *idea*.
3. The idea, when focused upon, considered, shared, or collaborated on with others over time builds and turns into a *desire* for its achievement.
4. When we desire something long enough and passionately enough, it becomes a part of us. This gradually builds the beginnings of *belief* in what it is that we desire, which also builds belief in our own ability to achieve or have what we desire. (I *think* I can do it.)
5. When we intensely focus on what we desire, this increases our excitement and enthusiasm for what we desire, which, in turn, increases and expands our belief. This gradually builds and plants the first seeds of *faith*. This refers to both faith in what we desire as well as faith in our own ability to achieve it. (I *trust* I can do it.)
6. When we have even the smallest measure of faith in what we desire, this leads to taking small steps of *action*.
7. When we take the first steps of action, there is a natural corresponding increase in our desire.
8. This increase in desire deepens our belief as well as expands our faith.
9. This increase in our belief and faith leads to a corresponding increase in action in an effort to achieve what we desire. The more action we take toward the attainment of our desire, the more our

desire will increase and the more belief and faith we will have, which in turn leads to ever-increasing action.

10. This increase in action leads to ever-increasing desire and belief and an ever-expanding faith, which leads to an explosion of action that cannot be denied, held back, or stopped.

It is important to understand that the primary driver of change in your life is found in building the desire, belief, and faith necessary to take action. With consistent and persistently increasing desire, belief, faith, and action, we ultimately carry out and accomplish what was once nothing more than a fleeting thought or a passing notion.

This is the *magic formula,* which knowingly or unknowingly has been applied and carried out by everyone who has ever achieved anything of substance in their life.

The diagram below demonstrates this process.

Use this formula as a tool for understanding the logistical process that takes you from the smallest of inspirations or thoughts and ideas to achieving anything you may desire in your life. Know that nothing truly meaningful in life is ever achieved without building desire, belief, and faith, followed by massive action.

"Ideas are a dime a dozen.
People who implement them are priceless."
—Mary kay Ash

It is interesting that when we want to achieve something in our lives, most people never move very far past the desire phase. Taking the first critical steps toward your goal with belief in your mind and faith in your heart can often be all that is necessary to get the ball rolling toward taking action and the ultimate completion of what we desire. Once we take even the smallest steps of action, this can initiate a "snowball" effect, which, if repeated, is the foundation necessary for ever-increasing desire, belief, faith, and action.

Of course, nothing is ever accomplished by merely wanting or wishing for something. Nothing meaningful is ever accomplished in our lives until we build enough desire, belief, and faith to take action. Know that desire without *action* is nothing more than a wish or a daydream.

One of my longtime mentors is my very good friend Howard Partridge. Howard is an ultra-successful small business owner and business coach who has the unique ability to reduce complex problems into their simplest forms. Howard refers to the inability of people to put their ideas into action as F.T.I. or "Failure To Implement." He teaches that the failure to implement one's ideas (failure to take action) is the number one reason for business and personal failure. In the vast majority of cases, we already know what to do, but for some reason, we just don't do it.

I have a long-held belief that there are only three reasons people fail to achieve an objective. They either don't know *what* to do, they don't know *how* to do it, or they *choose* not to do it. I know it sounds crazy that someone would actually know *what* needs to be done and even know *how* to do it, but it just lies right there in the same pile with all the other things that they *coulda, woulda, shoulda* done.

What possible reason could there be for someone who has what they believe to be a true desire for something to not follow through and take the action necessary to accomplish it? What causes people to be so seemingly passionate about wanting to achieve something, and yet they never build the belief and faith necessary to take action and see it through?

Could it be *fear* that causes this? Sure, that could be a big part of it. There are many different types of fear. For most people, the fear of loss or the fear of failure can be debilitating. For some, fear of the unknown or the fear of change is enough to cause them to abandon what they consider to be the strongest of desires.

Could it be a lack of available time that keeps us from achieving our goal? Sure, most of us are far too busy these days, and our schedules always seem to be full.

Could it be a lack of confidence that keeps people from taking action? Absolutely! Most people live with self-doubt, and some have no idea why or where it comes from, it just consumes them.

Could it be a lack of specialized knowledge or a lack of money that holds them back? More than likely yes, these are very common issues.

Could it be that what stifles people is any one of a thousand *"reasons"* that keep them from achieving their goal? I'm positive this is the case, but there is only one problem. If you were to ask anyone who has ever achieved anything of substance in their life, they would without exception tell you they had to overcome a multitude of these so-called *reasons* to be successful. In-fact, some, including me, would argue that they were successful *because* of their challenges, not merely in spite of them. One of my favorite quotes on this subject is from the multi-billionaire co-founder of Oracle, Larry Ellison who quipped, "I have had all of the disadvantages required for success."

What we are talking about here covers all areas of life. This could be a battered wife who needs to get out of a dangerous home life but fears leaving as much as staying. This could be someone who suffers in poverty and would benefit from an education to rise above it but has convinced themselves that it's just too hard or that education is a privilege reserved for *others*. It could be a teenager who has a bright future ahead of them but seeks the approval of friends instead of dedicating themselves to their schoolwork, thus sabotaging their future. And yes, it could also be a young entrepreneur who has an innovative idea that never gets off the ground because they wrongly believe that no one will take them seriously because they are working out of a college dorm room or their parents' garage. Imagine what would the world look like today without this type of start that Bill Gates, Michael Dell, Mark Zuckerberg, and Steve Jobs all have in common?

Understand this and drive this into your soul: Success and the accomplishment of your goals are not determined by where you come from or what your family is like. Your success is not determined by how bleak your current economic situation is. It is completely irrelevant how well you did in school, what religion you practice, what gender you are, what race you are, or where you come from. You can take off the list almost any other so-called *reason*, which might present itself along the way.

Some will argue that being successful or getting ahead in life is strictly for the affluent or the privileged few, and the deck is somehow stacked against those less fortunate. They believe that it doesn't matter how hard they work or how much they persist, they will never be able to get ahead or achieve what they desire in life. Well, I have news for you. Those individuals who are born into privilege can actually be among the most unfortunate of us all because of the atrophy and complacency it fosters. Being born into abundant wealth is every bit as much of a hurdle to true success and living an excellent and balanced life as almost anything else you could name. It is simply a different set of circumstances and obstacles to be recognized, understood, and overcome.

Almost nothing you can think of is an actual reason for not achieving what you desire in life. There are just too many examples of those who have overcome a multitude of overwhelming challenges and obstacles and go on to enjoy enormously successful, joyful, and excellent lives.

Your number one concern at this point should be in building the highest possible level of *desire, belief, faith,* and *action* behind what it is you want to accomplish. Do this, and you will develop an unshakable commitment to overcoming any obstacle that will undoubtedly present itself during the journey.

You see, we all have a choice in how we *choose* to view our circumstances. We can choose to look at what might seem to be a disadvantage as something that would prevent us from achievement, or we can choose to view the circumstance as merely an obstacle, which is an opportunity to grow stronger or become more creative because of it.

The truth is that we all have ideas that could improve our lives and desires to put into action. Just know that the foundational difference between those who succeed and carry their ideas to completion and those who do not lies in what happens *after* they take the initial steps of action and meet the first few obstacles. In the vast majority of cases, shortly after attempting to implement our ideas and running into *resistance*, we begin to justify to ourselves why it can't be done… or even worse, why *we* can't do it. When this happens, it simply means there is not enough *belief*, and *faith*, behind the desire.

It may be interesting to know that it doesn't matter what your desire is or even how large or small it might be. The only thing that is important at this point is having a *specific* desire of what it is you want to accomplish and building enough *belief* and *faith* in your own ability to get it done. Absolutely *nothing* else matters.

There is a definite and logistical process to all achievement, which is as follows:

1. **Desire.** Desire is your reason for getting out of bed. The foundation of your desire is *why* you want to accomplish your goal. It is fundamentally important to know that most people never get past simply having a casual desire for something, and they somehow convince themselves that their desire is stronger than it actually is. Know that how far you carry out what you

desire will be in direct proportion to how deeply you desire it or how much you want it.

2. **Belief & Faith.** Without a rock-solid *belief* in what you are attempting to accomplish, you will not get past first base. Belief is the fuel for what we desire. Without complete and total *belief*, which gradually and progressively transforms into absolute *faith* in what you desire, the desire itself is fruitless and meaningless.

3. **Action.** Action is the natural result of a true desire combined with a high level of belief, which builds into an unquestioned faith. Action is what gives life to what it is that you truly desire, unquestionably believe, and have full and complete faith in.

Before we go any further, let's look at desire, belief / faith, and action in detail and examine each very closely.

Desire

A desire is simply a strong feeling of wanting or wishing for something. I think it goes without saying that just because we want or wish for something doesn't mean we should have it or that we should spend our time, effort, energy, and resources pursuing it.

It is important to understand that casually desiring or wanting something is not enough for us to accomplish meaningful goals. And, by the way, we are not talking about desires such as what you want for dinner or what movie you wish to see. It is also important to point out that we are not discussing absurd desires, such as a 500-pound man desiring to be a horse jockey or an eighty-year-old man wanting to be an NFL quarterback.

Our purpose here is in addressing the major choices we all face and make in our lives. There are a multitude of things that we may *desire*, which, if achieved, would be very destructive to us. Because of this, it is important to know where our desires come from and most importantly *why* we desire them.

It is my belief that to take our desires to fruition, we must have a fundamental understanding of specifically *what* we want as well as fully understanding *why* we want it. Knowing *why* we want something can often be more revealing to us than *what* we want because it exposes our true motives. For this reason, it's important to examine every aspect of what it is that you desire so you have complete clarity about *why* you want it.

By closely examining the *what* and *why* behind your desire, it is important to make sure it is void of pride or selfishness. There is almost nothing that can cause us to stumble faster or harder than pride, and we seldom, if ever, realize our own selfish nature until it has caused us to suffer loss or go through great pain. It is for this reason, that we must approach what it is we desire with a humble heart and sincere motives, which are meant for the benefit of others as well as ourselves.

> *"When you ask, you do not receive because*
> *you ask with wrong motives."*
> *—James 4:3, NIV*

I have learned that before approaching anything of substance, I need to talk with God about my desires. Take refuge in the fact that there is nothing we can want, need, or desire that God doesn't intimately understand because He is the architect, author, and creator of everything that we are.

Going through this process will infinitely increase your desire and build an unwavering confidence that your desires will not only have God's blessing but also His unquestioned leadership, which will fuel what comes next... *belief* and *faith*.

Belief and Faith

Where I come from, there is a saying: "You don't get nothin' unless you ask for it." I imagine this expression has its roots in Matthew 7:7–8. To have a true desire for something that is well beyond the ordinary is what gives our lives passion, meaning, and purpose. However, it's not nearly enough to just ask for what you desire because nothing will happen unless you have a high level of belief and unquestioned faith. Passionately pursuing something we truly desire can be what ignites that fire in our gut and causes us to expand our vision of what we believe is possible for our lives. This can often be the catalyst for us to achieve amazing things, but it will go nowhere without intense *belief* and absolute *faith*.

All things are possible to him who believes. Mark 9:23b, BSB

What does *belief* mean to you? A simple dictionary definition of belief is "to have trust or confidence in someone or something." Or, it is "an opinion or judgment in which a person is fully persuaded." When we say we have *belief*, in this case, we are saying we are fully persuaded and have trust and confidence in the knowledge that we can achieve or have what it is we desire.

If you look up the definition of *faith* you get pretty much the same answer as with belief. Belief and faith are very much interrelated and are often used interchangeably. The difference between the two is subtle but absolutely substantial. You can have belief without having faith, but you can never have faith without first having belief. In other words, with belief, you know it in your mind; with faith, you know it in your heart, which is where our true passions reside.

Hebrews 11:1 (NIV) tells us, "...faith is confidence in what we hope for and assurance about what we do not see." The most basic definition of faith is to believe in something that you cannot prove. It is important to understand that you must believe in something long before you have faith in it. We can often *believe* in something simply because we want to believe, but *faith* is much deeper than that. Faith comes from deep down inside of us. You can believe in something and still have doubt, but with faith, there is no doubt. We can have a desire for something and even have belief, but it will go nowhere until true and absolute faith is developed.

"Faith is taking the first step even when
we don't see the whole staircase."
–Dr. Martin Luther King, Jr.

When there is something in our hearts and minds that we desire, it can often come to us in degrees, like turning up the temperature on a stove, one notch at a time. As our desire for what we want increases, and we add to it even the tiniest amount of belief, it causes us to take incremental steps of action toward achieving what we desire. The addition of even the smallest steps of positive action will cause a corresponding increase in our desire, which in turn will increase our belief.

This process, when repeated, causes our mere *belief* to transform into the beginnings of *faith*. As we build our faith to a point where we possess absolute faith that we can have or achieve what we desire, this gives us a firm and unshakeable resolve, which in turn gives us the push we need to continue forward with ever-increasing action.

At the point where our mere *belief* transforms into absolute *faith*, belief and faith, in tandem, take on a life of their own, becoming an independent entity—standing alone, completely separate, and with the firmest of foundations.

When we take action, the process is recycled, moving it all forward. But it can't stop there. We have to keep moving forward, day after day, in the direction of attaining what it is we desire. As soon as we stop or even pause, we are not standing still, we are actually moving backward, moving farther away from what it is we desire.

You see, the smallest bit of action is all it takes to move forward, but it is vital to move forward. Forward to what? Forward to more desire, which leads to more belief, which leads to more faith and, thus, more action. It is important to understand that the tiny bit of action we develop at this point is not really the *action* that pushes us through to accomplish what we desire. The action at this stage is merely laying the foundation underneath what we desire.

Understand that the first bit of action is nothing more than a proving ground that merely validates and stabilizes the desire, belief, and faith. The vast majority of us assume that because we did *something*, this qualifies as *action*. And while doing something is far better than doing nothing, it in no way should be confused with the action necessary to accomplish your desire.

As Ernest Hemingway once warned, "Never mistake motion for action." Laying a foundation for our desires through small actions is what builds our desire and belief, which in turn increases our faith. It is like first dipping your toe into a pool of water that eventually builds the desire, belief, and faith necessary to take action and dive in headfirst.

There is a saying in the military: "No battle plan ever survives contact with the enemy." Well, the *enemy* here is ourselves… or as the famous "Pogo" cartoon declared, "I have met the enemy, and he is us." We are indeed our own worst enemy. Why? Because we tend to *overestimate* our internal desire and *underestimate* the amount of action it will take to achieve what we desire.

Understand that desire, belief, faith, and action are not events; rather, they are all individual parts of an ever-evolving process. None of this happens like the flip of a switch; it happens in ever-increasing increments. We incrementally increase our desire; we incrementally increase our belief; we incrementally increase our faith, and we incrementally increase the amount of action we put into achieving what we desire. Like laying bricks, one atop another and woven together, we incrementally build a solid foundation underneath what we desire, which in turn increases our *desire*, which increases our *belief* to a point where we have true and absolute *faith*. This is the necessary foundation for unleashing what comes next—massive *action*.

Action

One of my favorite quotes on this subject is from Dorothea Brande's classic book, *Wake Up and Live*, first published in 1936. The basis of this classic work is, "Act as if it were impossible to fail." To me, these words sum up the *attitude* with which we should approach every positive desire we have for our lives.

Ask yourself this question: How would your life be better if you approached every positive desire you have with the attitude that "It's impossible to fail"? Far too often, we approach our desires with the opposite frame of mind. We often approach what it is that we desire by being timid or tentative in an attempt to play it safe. What Dorothea Brande is pointing out is what Albert Einstein understood when he said, "In order to succeed, your desire for success must be greater than your fear of failure."

Acting as if it's impossible to fail pushes aside fear, lack of confidence, worry, anxiety, apprehension, and changes the focus of our minds from *"I can't"* to *"I can."* This positions our thoughts where they should be—on *action* and on fearlessly and relentlessly moving forward!

Think about what Isaac Newton said, "For every action, there is an equal and opposite reaction." This universal law points out that you can never get more out of something than you put into it. It also reminds us that we can achieve nothing without first paying the price. Understand that the only way for you to achieve what you desire in life is for you to put enough *action* behind your desire, and the only way you will ever achieve the appropriate level of action is by first building the necessary *desire*, *belief*, and *faith*.

Most seem to get stuck somewhere between *desire* and *action*. They want to convince themselves and others that they are working on what they desire with a high level of belief and faith, but the amount of action they put into what they desire does not reflect it, not understanding that our lack of action *reveals* our lack of desire, belief, and faith.

Many find themselves "stuck," unable to move forward, not realizing or understanding the basic and simple fact that what is necessary for them to move forward is simply to take *action*, and to continually move forward in the direction of what it is they want to accomplish.

With belief and faith, expand your vision of what is possible for your life. Know in your heart that an excellent life is about living with strength and fortitude, not about retreating, surrendering, or giving in to worry or fear.

Like David stood before Goliath with nothing but a sling and a rock, know that you have it within you to face down and overcome the giants in your own life.

Know that when you are inspired by a thought that captures your imagination, and you foster it into an idea, which becomes an all-consuming desire that fuels your belief and builds into undeniable faith and unrelenting action, that all true accomplishment is formed and completed in this process.

This is indeed the bedrock foundation of all true accomplishment and achievement in our lives.

The Big Idea

- All achievement begins with a thought,
  which gradually turns into an idea.
- Desire for something gradually builds necessary belief and faith.
- Nothing meaningful is ever accomplished without massive action.

Chapter 20
Time versus Achieving What We Desire

*"Time is a created thing. To say, I don't have time
is the same as saying I don't want to."*
–Lao Tzu, Chinese Philosopher

YOU can tell a lot about someone by how they spend their money, and the same is true about how they choose to spend their time because this ultimately reveals their priorities. It is simple: where you spend most of your *time* is where you place the most *value*. For this reason, I encourage you to sit down and take the time necessary to make an honest assessment of what is most important to you in your life.

It is interesting that the things we tend to see as being most valuable to us are actually not. Homes, cars, possessions, and even our careers can all be replaced, but what is most valuable to us can never be replaced. Our health, our children, families, friends, and our relationship with God are all priceless and could never be replaced, but does this accurately reflect how we spend our *time?*

I would encourage you to go back and revisit the chapters "Self-Awareness and Self-Observation" and "We Become What We Think About." Know that how we spend our time is a *choice* and, therefore, should be carried out in an intentional and deliberate way, based on the priorities we have established for our lives—our most important needs, beliefs, and values.

Let's face it, we all have a clean slate when we come into this world, and the only appointment we have on the day we are born is our eventual date with death, and we obviously have no control over that. What we do have control over, once we reach the age of understanding, is every single day in between, and the way we choose to spend every minute of our time is completely up to us.

Let me ask this question: Is there a difference between what you set out to accomplish in your life and the course you are currently on?

Keeping in mind that *success* is defined as "the realization of a premeditated goal," ask yourself these questions:

- What do you want to accomplish with your life?
- Are you on track to accomplish what you have chosen to do?
- If not, then why?
- Is the course you are currently on an intentional and deliberate course, or did it just kind of happen, gradually evolving to what it is today?
- Why do you have the job that you do?
- Why do you have the friends that you have?
- How did you end up at the point you are in your life?
- Is the path you are currently on a result of your having a premeditated plan or simply by random chance?

In his book, *Man's Search for Himself,* psychologist Dr. Rollo May wrote, "In our society, the opposite of courage is not cowardice; it is conformity." He points out that we tend to conform to the actions, choices, and opinions of those around us instead of intentionally and deliberately deciding for ourselves what direction we should take in life and earnestly knowing *why* we make the choices and decisions we do. I believe, as Earl Nightingale points out in his classic work, *The Strangest Secret,* that Dr. May refers to this as *cowardice* because when we conform, we are actually conforming to the wrong group. We conform to the group that is *easiest* for us to conform to and the one that is most likely to take our lives in the wrong or a negative direction. We tend to conform to the thoughts and behaviors of the vast majority of those around us who don't really have a detailed plan for their lives. We conform to those who do not have real and concrete goals and who have no real understanding of what they truly believe or value most.

Understand this… It is not until we have a clear understanding of *why* we think the way that we do and know exactly where our beliefs come from that we can understand why we are on the course we are on.

You see, the *key,* or *secret,* to having mastery over our time is not merely about managing the minutes or hours of our day. It is actually about having mastery over *ourselves* and over how we *allow ourselves* to spend our time.

When you have a specific and detailed plan for your life and you know specifically *why* you want to accomplish your aims, you find it much easier to make decisions about how to spend your *time.* Simply put, a task or project either fits into or advances your plans, priorities, beliefs, and values, or it does not.

It is *because* we become what we think about that we continually move in the direction *of* what we think about. If your mind is truly fixed on the most important areas of your life, then when something comes up that has the potential to derail or get in the way of this, we have an easier time saying *no* and not allowing ourselves to give in to the random things that just kind of "pop up." If, however, our thoughts are *not* fixed on the specific and most important areas of our lives, then when random tasks present themselves, we will, by default, take action on the random tasks.

If your mind does not have a specific direction to move in, it will, by default pick up on the random events or thoughts that present themselves throughout your day—either positive or negative—and your focus then turns to taking on these random, unplanned and unprioritized tasks, which ultimately accomplishes little to nothing, wasting your time or even taking your life in the wrong direction.

We *feel* busy because we *are* busy. Busy doing what? We are busy doing all the small, random, unplanned, and un-prioritized tasks we take on, one after another, to the point of being overwhelmed, anxious, and exhausted. When this happens, our minds feel conflicted, which leads to our becoming frustrated and confused. Then we get down on ourselves and wonder why we cannot move forward in life and achieve more. As a result, we experience the effects of "quiet desperation" and "aimless distraction" in our lives. This causes us to look at ourselves and wonder, "how could I possibly do any more than I am doing?" Those around us see how endlessly busy we are and think the same, but deep inside ourselves, we know the truth is much different. We know we are fully capable of being and doing much more, but we just don't know *how* to start or even *where* to begin. This can lead to a feeling of frustration and disappointment with ourselves because we are so completely overwhelmed and exhausted from doing empty tasks that merely occupy our time and ultimately accomplish nothing of any real or lasting importance.

So, we all have a choice. We can intentionally choose to spend our time on the most important areas of our lives, which move us in a positive direction. We can choose to focus our time on things that move our lives in a negative direction. Or we can do as the vast majority and choose nothing, which means that our lives—and, by default, the time we possess in our lives—will be filled with trivial, random, or low-priority tasks. As a result, we will achieve nothing of any real importance with our *time*.

For this reason, it is imperative to firmly establish your priorities and know *what* you believe and *why* you believe it, as well as to know precisely *what* you want to accomplish with your life and *why* you want to accomplish it. With this done, you will learn to quickly and almost instinctively evaluate different tasks and situations as they come up. These different tasks and situations either fit into advancing the priorities you have established for your life, or they do not. If they *do* fit, then simply prioritize them accordingly and take care of them, as you should. If they *do not* fit into your priorities, just set them to the side and focus on the most important areas of your life. This is the key, or secret, to accomplishing more in life by doing less.

When we firmly establish our priorities and set our minds on the most important areas of our lives, we are better able to set aside the trivial and random tasks, which leaves productive time for us to focus on the more meaningful goals. This, in turn, leads to a much higher level of satisfaction and accomplishment.

Sometimes, we have the desire to accomplish something specific, and we may even feel a real sense of urgency to accomplish it, but upon further examination, we realize that while it is indeed an important priority, it is simply not the right time in our lives to take on that task. This could be starting a business, going back to school, buying a home, having children, or any other meaningful goal. But we know in our hearts it is just not the right time in our lives for us to begin this particular journey. This could be something that we choose to hold onto for a more appropriate time in our future.

Remember that we have no choice but to "become what we think about." For this reason, in the absence of a _specific_ desire, our minds will take on random thoughts. This leads to wasting valuable time and falling into the confusion, anxiety, and frustration that goes on all around us.

On the other hand, if our minds _are_ focused on the areas of our lives that are truly most important to us—God, family, career, finances, intellectual pursuits, our physical well-being, friends, and personal pursuits—we naturally move closer to these things when this is where we _intentionally_ and _deliberately_ place our focus. These areas become the focus of how we spend our time.

As a result, when we focus on an area of our lives that is truly important to us, we are able to give it our _total_ and _complete_ attention. So, when we focus on God, we become godlier and grow closer to Him. When we focus on our families, we have a closer, stronger, and more loving family. When we make our job a priority and place full effort within each hour of every working day, we move forward in our careers. When we focus on our finances, we gain security and financial freedom. When we feed our minds, we gain knowledge, wisdom, and insight. When we focus on our physical health and make it a priority, we live a healthier, longer, and more productive life. When we purposefully focus on developing close friendships, this leads to more loving and close relationships. And when we have time for ourselves, we can fully and completely relax and enjoy the life that we have established for ourselves.

We indeed become what we think about, but this is to our advantage *only* when we demonstrate the wisdom to first establish the proper priorities in our lives and have the perspectives necessary to know what areas of our lives are most important and truly deserve our *time* and our focus. When we do this, we achieve the peace of mind necessary to fully enjoy the minutes, hours, and years of our lives in comfort, contentment, peace, and freedom.

The Big Idea

- How we spend every minute of our time is a *choice*.
- Focus your time on the top priorities in your life.
- Learn to say no to tasks that are not important.

Chapter 21
The Motivation Lie

WE all have goals we want to accomplish. As we have learned, the foundation of any goal is formed when we have an inspiration, which leads to a thought, and that thought turns into an idea, which ultimately consumes our minds.

We daydream about what the achievement of the goal might be like. Our enthusiasm causes us to stay up late into the evening, plotting and planning. We even lose sleep. The new goal gives us a renewed sense of purpose and something exciting to look forward to. The only issue is that for some strange reason, we just can't seem to find a way to get started.

In the chapter, *"Turning Thoughts and Ideas into Action,"* we discussed the logistical process that takes place when we have an inspiration or thought about what we want to accomplish. We covered each important step in specific detail. The initial inspiration or thought becomes an idea, the idea gains traction and turns into a desire, the desire builds into belief, which expands into faith, which leads to taking massive action, all the way through to its completion. But isn't there still something missing?

We have talked about the three basic reasons we fail to achieve what we want to accomplish.

> We either don't know what to do,
> we don't know how to do it,
> or we choose not to.

Let me say those last four words again:

... we choose not to.

Does our failure to take action really mean we are *choosing* to not take action, and if this is a choice, is this a conscious or an unconscious choice... or could it possibly be *both*?

It just doesn't seem logical that there is something we want to accomplish that excites us, even causes us to lose sleep, and yet we just can't seem to find a way to follow through and make it happen. Does this sound familiar? What is it that keeps us from accomplishing something for which we seem to have such enthusiasm and passion? How do we move beyond merely *thinking* about what we want to accomplish and move forward to taking action and getting it done? What is this small but vital missing ingredient that we so desperately need but can't quite seem to find or wrap our minds around?

What "Zone" Are You In?

We have already listed a whole host of *reasons* that could prevent us from achieving what we desire. First, there is fear. That is the fear of loss, fear of failure, fear of the unknown, and fear of change, among others. Then there is what we believe we *lack*. This could be the lack of confidence, a lack of specialized knowledge, the lack of money, the lack of time, and so on.

I am sure we could make an endless list of anything and everything that could present a roadblock, preventing us from achieving the important goals we have established within our lives, but the interesting thing is that these lists would most likely *not* include the actual cause for us not achieving our goals.

So, what is this missing task or piece of information that has the potential to change our lives and alter our behavior in a manner that would allow us to achieve whatever goals we establish for our life? As simple as it sounds, most people do not achieve the goals they set out to accomplish because they do not move out of (or far enough out of) their *comfort zones.*

> *"If you want something you've never had,*
> *you must do something you've never done."*
> *–Thomas Jefferson*

Inspiration, thought, idea, desire, belief, faith, and action, where does moving out of your "comfort zone" fit into this? Understand that moving out of your comfort zone should happen incrementally but also quite naturally—somewhere between moving from the *belief* and *faith* phase into the *action* phase. In fact, doing things that require us to move beyond what is easy and comfortable should be among our first meaningful steps of action.

It is these small bits of action that gradually, incrementally, and ever so slowly move us beyond the boundaries that we place on ourselves. Understand that it is these very boundaries that we feel keep us safe and secure that actually prevent us from meaningful accomplishment. It is this *safe zone*, the place where we feel the most comfortable and secure, that forms the walls which limits our accomplishments, stifles our growth, imprisons our future and robs us of our dreams. It is mandatory for you to know that for you to take the action necessary to accomplish any goal which you establish for your life, no matter how large or small, you have got to first find a way to knock down, destroy, or at least expand and continually reposition these self-imposed boundaries. Understand that this can only be accomplished through finding it within yourself to *do* what makes you uncomfortable and to do so with a correct and focused state of mind.

What exactly is our comfort zone? Alasdair White points out in his book, *From Comfort Zone to Performance Management*, that we operate from three different and distinct "zones." These are our "comfort zone," the "optimal performance zone," and the "danger zone," as outlined in the following graph.

White explains, "A comfort zone is a psychological state in which things feel familiar to a person, and they are at ease and in control of their environment, experiencing low levels of anxiety and stress."

It is an ironic fact that it is the act of *doing* what makes us *uncomfortable* that allows us to grow, expand our horizons, and move forward. Thus, following through and actually **_doing_** what makes us uncomfortable is what perfectly positions us to achieve the important goals we have established for our lives.

The way the human mind works is to have us avoid what makes us uncomfortable. Quite simply, our brains are wired to protect us from uncomfortable or "dangerous" things, and this is why we feel stressed and anxious when we attempt something new or out of the ordinary. Any time we venture outside of our comfort zone, we can feel as if we might be in the danger zone, but this is not the case in the vast majority of instances. Despite how we may *feel*, we are actually in our optimal performance zone, which, by definition, will always be a little uncomfortable.

The optimal performance zone is, in fact, optimal because this is where we feel a certain amount of elevated, yet *manageable*, anxiety and stress. We feel anxious and stressed because we are faced with doing things or acting in a manner to which we are unaccustomed, and this makes us uncomfortable or anxious. It is important to understand that this act *of doing* what makes us uncomfortable is what stimulates the inner growth necessary to move forward. With the correct perspective, it is when we feel (but are not overwhelmed by) anxiety and stress that we are most attentive and alert. It is during this phase, or in this zone, that we can experience increased focus and a heightened level of attention, which increases our interest, drive, and enthusiasm.

It is when we continually test, push, and reset the boundaries of our comfort zones (without actually pushing through into the danger zone) that we expand and increase our performance and, therefore, increase the amount of action we put behind our desires.

This takes intentional focus because we are simply not built to do what makes us anxious, stressed, or uncomfortable, so how we *choose* to respond to this additional anxiety and stress then becomes the issue.

When we are confronted with a situation in which we feel uncomfortable and anxious, our minds respond, causing us to hesitate. This hesitation can then lead to an additional elevated level of anxiety or stress, which results in conflicting messages, which are to *move ahead* or to *retreat*. When these conflicting messages occur, our minds tend to *magnify* the level of risk, or "danger," and your mind does everything possible to keep you away from what it perceives to be risky or dangerous.

What We Do Next Is the Key

When we are faced with a challenge that falls outside our comfort zones, our minds tell us to *stop*. We are built to "fight or flight," and our intended positive actions and our sincere best intentions can be overridden or sabotaged by our own internal thoughts. This can be when our emotions take over, and we start to focus on what we *fear* and what we may have to lose instead of focusing on our goals and what we have to gain.

When this happens, when the focus of our mind is changed from what we *want* to accomplish to what we fear *could* happen, we begin to allow self-doubt to enter our thoughts and minds. We begin to tell ourselves how difficult our goal will be to achieve. We begin the process of counting the obstacles in our path. We attempt to convince ourselves it is not worth the price we will have to pay or that the goal is not meant for us to achieve. We then rationalize why we should not push forward and justify to ourselves and others why we should scale back or even abandon the goal. This is when we metaphorically go through life with one foot on the gas and one foot on the brake. This is, in fact, the root cause of most failures.

What we need are confidence and courage. But what our minds deliver is the opposite. Without immediate *action* to the contrary, this causes us to make incremental decisions to play it safe, which offers less risk, and are more comfortable. As a result, we begin to lose focus, we digress, and gradually retreat from the goal or downsize our expectations rather than move forward and experience growth.

As a result, our actions gradually become less focused and more aimless. We become more distracted and less interested in what we had once considered our passion. Because of this, we can take on feelings of guilt and even shame, instead of the excitement and enthusiasm we had anticipated and had hoped to experience. We can then begin to pick back up those old bad habits which take our lives in the wrong or negative direction.

One day, we wake up and ask ourselves, "How did I get here?" We wonder how to get back to where we know in our hearts we should be. This is when we face the fact that we know *what* to do to accomplish our goal and even know *how* to do it, but we just can't seem to make ourselves *do* what is necessary to take action and accomplish the goal.

The simple fact is that for you to achieve anything of importance in your life, it is going to be because you pushed yourself beyond the boundaries of your comfort zone. This can only be accomplished by using the anxiousness, apprehension, and stress you feel as *fuel to actually do what makes you uncomfortable.* As previously stated, when you are faced with a situation that makes you uncomfortable, your mind will send you a signal that causes you to feel anxious and stressed. You now have a choice. You can interpret this elevated feeling of anxiousness and stress as a signal that you should *stop*, or you can interpret this as a signal that you should *go*. You can use the anxiety and stress that you feel to rationalize and justify why you should retreat, or you can use this exact same anxiety and stress to surge ahead. Understand that this is all a *choice* and fully within your control.

Without immediate intervention, your mind will make a nearly instant *unconscious* choice, and this unconscious choice will nearly always be to retreat from the goal. To defeat this process and turn it around, you must form the new and positive habit of immediately overriding your initial thoughts and feelings of anxiety and stress, transforming them into enthusiasm and excitement, and allowing yourself to make the *conscious* choice of moving forward toward the goal.

The reason the title of this chapter is "The Motivation Lie" is because most people think they are not achieving their goals simply because they lack the proper motivation. And, while this may be partially true, you are never going to push yourself out of your comfort zone *far enough* or for *long enough* to accomplish meaningful goals because you are motivated to do so.

Don't get me wrong, motivation is important. I think it goes without saying that nothing of significance will happen in life unless you have the proper motivation, but also understand that motivation in and of itself is simply not enough. Motivation by itself is fleeting, has little depth, and is not sustainable.

What *does* last and what is ultimately necessary to achieve worthwhile goals is confidence, courage, strength of will, integrity, and fortitude. In addition to motivation, it is the formulation of positive habits and the building of positive character traits that lead to long-term success. This simply cannot be accomplished within the safety and security of our comfort zones.

If we were going to turn this into a mathematical equation, it would look like this:...

You can choose:

$$M + PH + PC = A$$

Motivation + Positive Habits + Positive Character = Achievement

Or you can choose:

$$M - PH - PC = F$$

Motivation - Positive Habits - Positive Character = Frustration.

Let me put this another way. It is the formulation of positive habits and the building of positive character traits that give us the necessary strength and confidence to do what had previously created enough anxiety or stress within us to cause inaction. It is only when we move in the direction of our fears that we are able to leave the safety and security of our comfort zones, cast aside our insecurities and doubts, and push through to a life of confidence, courage, and abundance. Know that long-term success, which is predictable and sustainable, can only be achieved by becoming the type of person who will diligently work to develop the inner strength and fortitude necessary to move beyond what is convenient and comfortable.

It is imperative to understand that long-term and sustainable success is reserved for those who are willing to work to improve *themselves* in a manner that builds an outstanding work ethic, strength of will, strength of character, courage, fortitude, and integrity. Know that the deeper you develop these and other positive character traits into your life, and the more they become a part of *who you are*, the more predictable and sustainable your success and personal growth will become.

Let's face it...; achieving anything of significance is hard, sometimes unimaginably hard. Just think about it... How does someone earn a college degree, much less an MBA or a Ph.D.? How does someone build a business, start a ministry, become a world-class athlete, rise out of poverty, conquer an illness, face death in combat, defeat illiteracy, heal a broken family, get out of debt, or recover from addiction? These goals and endless others are achieved by those who are willing to do, not merely what is easy, convenient, or comfortable, but, what can be extremely difficult and highly uncomfortable.

Know that long-term, lasting success and an excellent life must be *earned*. It is earned by those who are inspired by a thought that captures their imaginations, which is then fostered into ideas that are transformed into all-consuming desires that fuel their beliefs, and transformed into unstoppable faith, and unrelenting action.

Those who succeed and ultimately achieve the chief aims of their lives do so because they find deep within themselves, the ability to move beyond the confines and boundaries of their comfort zone. They learn to embrace circumstances where they face risk and where they are forced to take on new and ever-increasing challenges. As a result, they become stronger and more capable, and their abilities, skills, and confidence are increased. They do this because it is the pathway to accomplishment, personal growth, and contentment. In return, they are granted rewards far beyond what they could have ever imagined. They do this even though it is initially uncomfortable, maybe even a little scary, and in every case, well beyond their comfort zone.

The Big Idea

- Motivation alone is not enough.
- Nothing meaningful happens within your comfort zone.
- Work to become comfortable doing the uncomfortable.

Chapter 22

Finish Well

*The way we respond to temptation
reveals the true nature of our character.*

ONE thing that always makes me cringe is hearing about someone who has "fallen." By "fallen," I mean someone who has achieved a certain level of success or respect in their life, and then they do something to severely damage it or throw it all away. You know what I mean—the athlete, politician, pastor, celebrity, law enforcement officer, schoolteacher, business or military leader, husband, wife, or parent who does something to destroy, not just their reputation, but in many cases, everything they have worked so hard and for so long to achieve.

Just think about all of those you have known of and heard about over the years that fall into this category. I don't have to name them; you know who they are, and you know what they have done. My aim here is not to magnify these individuals' mistakes or wag an accusing finger at them. My point is merely to discuss *why* this happens in the lives of so many in an effort to help you avoid this trap.

Dealing with Temptation and Building Our Character

How does it happen that a person can reach a certain level of success in life and then seem to severely stumble or even have their lives fall apart because they gave in to some type of avoidable temptation? I am sure that you have asked yourself why this happens in the lives of those who seem to have accomplished so much and have so much to lose. There are many reasons for this, and there is no single trap they all fall into, but the common denominator seems to be giving in to some type of negative temptation, revealing a lack *of* or causing a lapse *in* their character.

Wikipedia describes *temptation* as: "The desire to perform an action that one may enjoy immediately or in the short term but will probably later regret for various reasons such as legal, social, psychological (guilt) health or economic. Temptation is usually used in a loose sense to describe actions which indicate a lack of self-control."

> *"I can resist everything but temptation."*
> *—Oscar Wilde*

Let's face it, life can be tough, and there are endless distractions and temptations that can derail even the strongest and the best of us if we allow them to. So why is it that we are so vulnerable to temptation? I mean, one minute we are just minding our own business, and then out of nowhere, we see something or have a thought that tempts us to do what we know we should not. I'm not talking about stressing over something as simple as having a bowl of ice cream when we know that we need to lose weight. What I am discussing here are the larger issues of life that cause us to lie, cheat, steal, commit adultery, or anything similar.

It just seems that when we achieve a certain level of comfort or "success" in our lives, we tend to become more vulnerable to falling into the trap of thinking we can somehow write our own rules without having to endure the consequences. We attempt to convince ourselves that we have in some way earned the object of our temptation… and then we are trapped.

It doesn't matter if we are being tempted by an affair, money, power, the admiration of others, revenge, or our "vices." We somehow find a way to twist and contort our thinking to convince ourselves that the negative behavior is acceptable, rational, or even justified when it is anything but.

We want to believe we are flying under the radar and have everything under control when in reality, we are flying headlong into a self-imposed downfall. We try to convince ourselves that we won't get caught because we are too smart or too clever for that. The truth is that even if we have all of our bases covered and we manage to keep others from learning our secrets, we can't avoid the fact that *we* know what we have done, which can bring on damaging and destructive *guilt* and *shame*. Always remember that there are no secrets the passing of time will not fully reveal.

I have a self-imposed rule in my own life, which is "have no secrets." The rule I have for myself is: If I wouldn't do it in front of the world, including everyone I know, love, and care about most, then I just don't do it. When I am faced with a temptation, what I attempt to do is force myself to think about the consequences and everything I have to lose. I am in no way saying that this makes me immune to temptation because it most certainly does not. But doing this helps me to put the situation and the temptation in their proper perspective so that I am better armed to deal with the temptation.

It goes without saying that no temptation or selfish gratification is worth sabotaging our futures or hurting and disappointing the people we love and care about most. No matter how much we might think we "deserve" what we are tempted with, we are only fooling ourselves, and it is not worth it.

Understand that what we are discussing here is not about avoiding the *consequences* that surely come from giving in to what tempts us. What we are addressing here are the larger issues of *being in control* of ourselves instead of being *controlled by* our temptations. Our major focus here is placed on building positive habits, self-discipline, self-control, and, ultimately, mastery over the most important areas of our lives.

Ask yourself if what you are doing right now or have considered doing that has the potential to destroy what you truly love, value, and care about most. Consider your relationship with God, your family and friends, your personal reputation, and even your freedom. Is giving in to any negative temptation worth the risk of damaging or losing what is most important to you in your life? Of course not.

The ills of temptations can bind us all. This is the reason it is important to guard your thoughts and continually feed your mind with pure, powerful, and positive thoughts. This is why I continually point out that each one of us needs to *deliberately* decide *in advance* what we believe and know with absolute certainty *why* we have these beliefs. This is why we need to weed out and discard the impure areas of our lives and control what we *allow* to go into our minds. This is why we must set priorities in our lives and know with absolute certainty *why* we have those priorities. This is the reason we must know beyond any doubt *why* we make the choices and decisions we do and to understand the foundation of them. This is why we have to know way deep down inside of ourselves who we are, the type of life we should lead, and the legacy we will *choose* to leave behind. Know that living a truly excellent life is not possible unless we *deliberately* decide *in advance* what our lives will stand for and what we will defend to the end.

You see, when you decide in advance what your beliefs are, when you know way down deep in your heart exactly what your priorities in life are, when you know beyond any doubt what is most important to you, then when you are tempted by something that has the potential to derail you or to bring real harm in your life, you don't have to decide what to do in the middle of the temptation because *that decision has already been made.* You have already established, *in advance,* that you are a person of integrity. You have already decided, well before you are faced with the temptation, that you are a person of positive character. You have already made the decision that you will not compromise what you believe in and jeopardize what you love and value most.

Let's face it, we are all human, and in today's world, we are continually bombarded with every imaginable type of temptation. Because of this, we have to be continually aware that we are vulnerable to destructive temptations, such as envy, jealousy, greed, intolerance, anger, pride, as well as our vices, and we should have a solid plan based on our strengths and weaknesses to deal with them.

Remember, "We become what we think about." So, if we continually think about and dwell on what is tempting us, we will eventually *become what we are tempted by*. When we think about achieving revenge, we become vengeful. When we dwell on taking what is not ours, we become a thief. When we think about cheating on our spouse, we become an adulterer. And if we think about how we can lie and cover up the truth, we will ultimately become dishonest and untrustworthy.

"Talent is a gift, but character is a choice."
–John Maxwell

Everyone wants to end their time here on earth with their reputations and integrity intact. We want to live up to our full potential and be good examples for those who look up to us and who depend on us. We want to have *earned* the respect of those in our lives whom we love and care about most. We should never allow a time of temptation and weakness to interfere with that.

Make it a point to count your blessings. I mean physically sit down, grab a pen and paper, and make a list of everything in your life that you value and care about most. Take the time to assess your life and be thankful for what you have. Think about *in advance* what is most important to you. Consider those who have *not* done this and who have thrown their reputations or even their freedom away because they *forgot* or failed to fully understand what is most important.

We are all fully capable of self-reflection, and as a result, have conscious knowledge of our feelings, desires, and our actions. This gives us the ability to achieve awareness of the self-conscious emotions of guilt, shame, and pride. These characteristics are embedded within us *all* for one simple reason—so that we have the ability to continually build upon and improve our character.

God has given us the ability to fail, learn from our mistakes, and improve—to try again and again, and to be repeatedly tested. And with each test, we have the opportunity to learn and grow. It is through this process that we have the ability to learn from our mistakes, improve, and move forward to living richer, more satisfying, and rewarding lives.

The true nature of our character will always
be revealed within our struggles.

Dealing with temptations begins with continually building and strengthening our character and knowing ourselves in the most intimate and honest way. Do whatever it takes to know and understand your vulnerabilities. Be honest enough to admit to yourself what your weaknesses are and the areas of your character that need strengthening. Search to understand what you are tempted by, and make it a priority to purposefully avoid situations that can place you in temptation.

This is about patiently searching your heart and being completely truthful with yourself. This is about knowing yourself well enough to, beyond any doubt, understand where you are weak and where you are strong and using that information to build up and reinforce the areas of your character that are weakest. Be aware that if you are being truly tempted, it is because this is an area of your life where you are weak, and your character needs to be strengthened.

Make a sincere effort to learn from every circumstance in life and share what you have learned with others. Also, be mindful to notice positive traits in others. Seek out like-minded, wise, and seasoned mentors who can help you build a more solid foundation and who will hold you accountable.

Earnestly implementing this as a regular part of your daily life will make you infinitely stronger and less vulnerable to potentially destructive temptations. Know that you are never alone in your temptations, and there is always a way out of what is tempting you. God promises to always be with you. He intimately loves you, and He will never abandon you.

Understands that trials, tests, and temptations are an ongoing part of life. There will be times when we fall short, and the weakest areas of our character will be revealed to us through our repeated tempting thoughts. This requires that we are diligent in noticing even the smallest temptations as they enter our minds. Learn and build the positive habit of taking immediate action to put them behind you before you allow yourself to act on these negative temptations. Remember that actions repeated become habits. In this case, let your actions be in doing whatever is necessary to overcome and eliminate the temptation.

It is important to understand that life's greatest battles are not fought against some outside foe but are, in fact, fought *within ourselves* and against the unseen temptations and challenges to our character. When we have lapses of character we want to say to ourselves or others, "That's just how I am" or "I'm only human," not realizing or understanding that we hold the keys to the chains that shackle and bind us; we simply refuse to use them.

It is important to see temptations for what they are, *tests*, and as tests, they can be overcome and conquered. It doesn't matter what your struggle is. It doesn't matter if you are tempted by a vice, such as alcohol, gambling, pornography, or drugs. It doesn't matter if you struggle with an overload of debt, an entanglement of lies, pride, greed, resentment, jealousy, selfishness, anger, laziness, bad or destructive relationships, or anything else. Know that they can all be dealt with, overcome, and defeated, and doing so is one hundred percent within your control.

Understand that *no one else can fight these battles or face these enemies for you.* You, and you alone, must muster the strength and fortitude necessary to face and defeat the negative issues in your life. Don't misunderstand. If there is a negative issue you are facing in your life that you need help with conquering, then *get help*; do whatever it takes to defeat it. But understand that no challenge in life can be overcome *for you* by others. Someone else cannot want something *for you* more than you want it for yourself. It is up to you to take the first step of action. You need to be the driving force behind any positive change in your life or it simply will not happen, and you will always struggle.

You can be sure that temptation will hit you the hardest when you least expect it and where you are most vulnerable. Understand that it is through making correct choices with the small and seemingly insignificant choices and decisions we face, day in and day out, that our character is either built and strengthened or slowly eroded.

Know that there is no standing still. Your character is either being strengthened by your diligent action to do so, or your character is being gradually eroded by neglect and lack of purposeful and intentional action in this area. There is no middle ground.

> *"Everyone must choose one of two pains in life,*
> *the pain of discipline or the pain of regret."*
> *–Jim Rohn*

Know that it is always easier to deal with the temptation rather than have to endure the consequences of giving in to it. Being disciplined in your approach to life in a way that continually builds your character is not easy and is a never-ending pursuit. In the beginning, it can often mean going through great pains to build the necessary positive habits and discipline to achieve self-control. But as you continually build and reinforce the positive habit of recognizing and dealing with the temptations you face; they will become easier to subdue and ultimately become less challenging to overcome.

As you implement these positive habits into your life, the depth of your character will improve. You will gradually become stronger and progress from simply giving in to what tempts you to forming new inner strength, self-control, self-confidence, and inner peace.

With continual focus and positive effort, over time, it will almost become second nature for you to cast aside the very temptations which had formerly bound you and held you back. The same negative issues that once consumed and shackled you will begin to drop away, almost without notice, and can ultimately be left solidly and firmly behind—though it is important to understand that the negative habits and temptations will *never* fully be laid to rest. Know that the seed of the negative temptation will always be with you, lying buried and dormant deep within, waiting to be regenerated with the potential to grow again.

Don't forget that *we alone* decide the level of involvement that we ultimately have in our own lives. When it comes to building a life of excellence, self-mastery, and increased character, there are only two plans:

Plan A is to take the reins of life in your hands and move in any positive direction that you intentionally and deliberately choose.

Plan B is to yield control of yourself to others and the endless random temptations and circumstances of life.

Sadly, the vast majority choose Plan B never realizing or fully understanding that a choice has been made at all… And don't attempt to fool yourself, there is no *Plan C*.

> **"Weakness of attitude becomes weakness of character."**
> **–Albert Einstein**

You can count on the fact that the more "success" you experience and the more abundance you realize in life, the more you will be tempted and the larger and more powerful the temptations you will face. This is where many of those who have experienced some measure of achievement, respect, or success in life ultimately backslide or even fail, sometimes irretrievably.

They falsely believe that the act of accomplishing their goals is enough and that they have finally "made it." They mistakenly assume or believe that because they have experienced a certain level of success, the success will simply continue without interruption. They falsely assume or believe that they are now somehow less susceptible or even immune to the challenges they once faced… and then they are tempted. This can often be the beginning of a series of ongoing struggles, which they may never fully understand, will often blame others for, and may never completely resolve or recover from.

We tend to believe there is no connection between the two. We fail to see what the achievement of our goals has to do with our character or our temptations. We want to tell ourselves that we can be one way at home and another way at work. We want to believe we can tell little lies or deceive those around us, and it won't matter—that there will be no meaningful or lasting consequences.

When we do this, when we allow ourselves to make exceptions of character, we begin to dig ourselves a hole by giving in to temptation. We start with a teaspoon and later take on a shovel, and we never see or realize the difference. We simply rationalize and justify the negative behavior and dig larger and deeper holes, never understanding how we are sabotaging ourselves, ultimately undermining our current and future ambitions and successes.

Know that you have the ability to choose your own fate. You have the power within you to master yourself and be in control of your own life. You see, you and you alone choose to follow good or evil. You are the one who chooses knowledge or ignorance. You are the one who seeks love or intolerance. You alone choose strength over weakness. You have the freedom to choose abundance or bondage. And yes, you and you alone choose discipline and self-control over the pain of regret that comes from giving in to temptation.

I challenge you to learn to look at your life from the *outside in* and to build your life from the *inside out*. Look at your life from God's perspective. Look at yourself with an eye toward your own heart and closely examine your true motives and the direction of your life. Choose to live a life filled with passion and wholeness, a life of no excuses and no regrets.

With honesty and integrity, set your own course in the direction you have intentionally chosen. Never allow life's temptations to get the best of you or to derail your future. Never allow a time of weakness to cause you to lose sight of what you dream about accomplishing. Never compromise your integrity or risk what you hold most dear. Never lose sight of what you truly love, cherish, and value most. Intentionally choose to live a life filled with boundless resolve, true and lasting strength of will, strength of heart, and strength of character. Make a deliberate and conscious choice to live *an excellent life*, and above all... finish well.

The Big Idea

- Everyone struggles with temptation.
- Acknowledge your temptations and understand what you have to lose.
- Choose to live an excellent life.

ENDNOTES

Chapter 1

Ellis, Linda, "The Dash," accessed February 19, 2021, https://thedashpoem.com/.

Chapter 3

Lewis, Clive Staples. *The Screwtape Letters*. New York: HarperCollins Publishers, 2001.

Chapter 5

Thoreau, Henry David. *Walden*. London: Dent, 1910.

Chapter 6

Ziglar, Zig. *Goals: How to Get the Most Out of Your Life*. Shippensburg, PA: Sound Wisdom Publishing, 2019.

Chapter 8

Forward, Susan. *When Your Lover is a Liar*. New York: Harper Perennial, 1999.

Shakespeare, William, 1564–1616. *A Midsummer Night's Dream*. New York: Signet Classic, 1998.

Chapter 10

Regarding the brain statistics... Burr, Shelby. "10 Unforgettable Statistics About Human Memory." Artifact. Accessed February

22, 2021, https://southtree.com/blogs/artifact/10-unforgettable-statistics-about-human-memory.

Chapter 13

Regarding Mayme White Miller's poem, "Yourself to Blame" and story of Sonya Carson and her children... Carson, Ben. *Gifted Hands*. Grand Rapids, MI: Zondervan, 1992.

Chapter 14

Tanner, Michael. "How Government Causes Poverty." *The Cato Institute*, Cato's Letter, Spring 2019, volume 17, no. 2., accessed February 22, 2021, https://www.cato.org/sites/cato.org/files/pubs/pdf/catosletter_spring2019.pdf.

Regarding rate of children born outside of marriage... Rector, Robert. "The War on Poverty: 50 Years of Failure." *The Heritage Foundation*, September 3, 2014, accessed February 22, 2021, https://www.heritage.org/marriage-and-family/commentary/the-war-poverty-50-years-failure.

Regarding poverty and middle-class statistics... Sawhill, Isabel V., et. al. "Pathways to the Middle Class: Balancing Personal and Public Responsibilities." The Brookings Institute, September 20, 2012, accessed February 22, 2021, https://www.brookings.edu/wp-content/uploads/2016/06/0920-pathways-middle-class-sawhill-winship.pdf.

Gladwell, Malcolm. *Outliers: The Story of Success*. New York: Back Bay Books, 2011.

The Annie E. Casey Foundation. *"Early Warning! Why Reading by the End of Third Grade Matters."* Baltimore: The Annie E. Casey Foundation, 2010. Accessed February 23, 2021, https://www.aecf.org/resources/early-warning-why-reading-by-the-end-of-third-grade-matters/.

Chapter 16

Brown University. "The Cost of the Global War on Terror: $6.4 Trillion and 801,000 Lives." Providence: Brown University, 2019. Accessed February 21, 2021, https://www.brown.edu/news/2019-11-13/costsofwar.

Regarding statistic about the death of one officer every fifty-four hours... National Law Enforcement Officers Memorial Fund, accessed February 19, 2021, https://www.charities.org/charities/national-law-enforcement-officers-memorial fund#:~:text=On%20 average%2C%20one%20law%20enforcement%20officer%20is%20 killed,1984%2C%20is%20a%20501%20%28c%29%20%283%29%20 nonprofit%20organization.

Regarding statistics about the death of firefighters... National Fire Protection Association, accessed February 19, 2021, https://www. nfpa.org/News-and-Research/Data-research-and-tools/Emergency-Responders/Firefighter-fatalities-in-the-United-States/Firefighter-deaths.

Chapter 17

Carlson, Richard. *Don't Sweat the Small Stuff.* Philadelphia: Hachette Books, 1997.

Mandino, Og. *The Greatest Salesman in the World.* New York: Bantum Doubleday Dell, 1972, reprint.

Chapter 18

Hogan, Chris. *Everyday Millionaires: How Ordinary People Built Extraordinary Wealth⊠and How You Can Too.* Nashville: Ramsey Press, 2019.

Chapter 19

Brande, Dorothea. *Wake Up and Live*. Hawthorne, CA: BN Publishing, 2014, educational reprint.

Chapter 20

May, Rollo. *Man's Search for Himself.* New York: W. W. Norton & Company, 2009, reprint.

Chapter 21

White, Alasdair. *From Comfort Zone to Performance Management.* Belgium: White & MacLean Publishing, 2009, Kindle.